Pennsylvania Battlefields & Military Landmarks

ARTHUR P. MILLER JR.

&

MARJORIE L. MILLER

STACKPOLE BOOKS

0 11557 02876 8

Front cover: *The Pennsylvania Memorial in Gettysburg National Military Park bears the names of all the soldiers from Pennsylvania who fought at Gettysburg.*
COURTESY OF AMERICANA SOUVENIRS AND GIFTS

Back cover: *Statue of George Washington at Fort LeBoeuf portrays him as he delivered his demand in 1753 that the French abandon their possessions in the Ohio River Valley. Washington is dressed as a major in the Virginia militia.*

Published by
STACKPOLE BOOKS
5067 Ritter Road
Mechanicsburg, PA 17055
www.stackpolebooks.com

Printed in the United States of America

10 9 8 7 6 5 4 3 2 1

FIRST EDITION

Cover design by Caroline Stover
Photographs by the authors, unless otherwise noted

Library of Congress Cataloging-in-Publication Data

Miller, Arthur P. Jr.
    Pennsylvania battlefields and military landmarks / Arthur P. Miller Jr. & Marjorie L. Miller.—1st ed.
        p. cm.
    Includes index.
    ISBN 0–8117–2876–5
    1. Historic sites—Pennsylvania—Guidebooks. 2. Battlefields—Pennsylvania—Guidebooks. 3. Military parks—Pennsylvania—Guidebooks. 4. Pennsylvania—History, Military. 5. Pennsylvania—Guidebooks. I. Miller, Marjorie L. (Marjorie Lyman), 1929– II. Title.

F150 .M57 2000
917.4804'43—dc21
                                                                99–056904

To all those battle reenactors who volunteer their time and share their talents as "weekend warriors" despite blazing sun, driving rainstorms, and snowy weekends to breathe life into our past. Their portrayals of historic events and people of all kinds give us first-person insights into the achievements and defeats that together make up the story of our country's military heritage.

Contents

ACKNOWLEDGMENTS

For us it has been a grand adventure, crisscrossing Pennsylvania for more than 5,000 miles to gather first-hand information to describe these military landmarks. Travelers who follow in our footsteps and relive the episodes represented by these sites will be the beneficiaries. If we have succeeded in casting new light on the state's rich heritage, we have many people to thank.

Donna Williams, Director of the Bureau of Historic Sites and Museums in Harrisburg, helped us define the scope of the book. It was her guidance and enthusiasm that laid the groundwork for our research.

As the adventure continued, others lent generously of their time and knowledge, sharing with us valuable information or materials: Brian Fitzgerald and John Heiser, Gettysburg National Military Park; Richard Lemmers, Eisenhower National Historic Site; Murray Kauffman, Chambersburg; Carolyn Stauffer, Hanover Area Historical Society; Larry Wallace, Hanover; John Giblin III, Fort Pitt Museum and Bushy Run Battlefield; Joanne Hanley, Fort Necessity National Battlefield; Martin West and Penny West, Fort Ligonier; Roy Frazier, Butler; Benjamin Holland, Evans City; Jane Richardson, Hunter House and Fort Augusta; Jack Hetrick, Northumberland County Historical Society; Anna Rotz, Fort Loudoun Historical Society; Chris Schillizzi, Phil Sheridan, and Karen Stevens, Independence National Historical Park; Peggy Goodman, Fort Roberdeau; Toni Collins, Washington Crossing Historic Park; Connie Stuckert, Brandywine Battlefield; Patrick McGuigan and Thomas McGuire, Paoli Battlefield Preservation Fund; Dori McMunn, Fort Mifflin; Kris Kepford, Cliveden; Lori Nygard, Fort Washington State Park; and Steve Miller, Hope Lodge.

Thanks also to John Slonaker and Louisa Arnold-Friend, U.S. Military History Institute; Bruce Stocking, Valley Forge National Historical Park; David Rowland, Old York Road Historical Society; Michael Bertheaud, Wyoming Historical and Geological Society; Myrna Hart, David Bradford House; Chris Magoc and Richard Liebel, Erie Maritime Museum and U.S. Brig *Niagara*; Randy Neyer, Presque Isle State Park; Edwin Morrison, Fort LeBoeuf Historical Society; Dr. Renata Wolynec, Fort LeBoeuf Museum; Michael Angelo, Independence Seaport Museum; Joseph Horvath, Pennsylvania Military Museum; Ron Gancas, Soldiers and Sailors Memorial Hall; Jack Hyland, Veterans of the Battle of the Bulge, Havertown; Maj. Gen. Frank Smoker, Jr., USAF (Ret.), Lebanon; Sgt. Maj. Warren Parks, USA (Ret.), Charles Oellig, and Lt. Col. Chris Cleaver, Fort Indiantown Gap; Scott Kleinschnitz, USS *Requin*; David Shaw, World War II Historical Preservation Federation; Robert Messner, Braddock Field Historical Society; Marianne Childress, The Great War Foundation; and Russell Strine, Mid-Atlantic Air Museum.

For their assistance in providing illustrations to enrich the text we are indebted to historical artist Robert Griffing of Gibsonia for permission to publish his "In the Shadow of the King," which depicts Fort Pitt; Jules Desgains, Verona; Charles Morrison, Garner, North Carolina; Tom Stolfi, Brandywine Battlefield State Park; Bruce Stocking, Valley Forge National Historical Park; Kelly McCann and David Jackson, Valley Forge Military Academy; and Michael Sherbon, Pennsylvania State Archives.

And finally, a bow to Kyle Weaver, our excellent editor at Stackpole Books, who worked with us so effectively to pull together this book that showcases our efforts and the contributions of all those above.

INTRODUCTION

Pennsylvania stands squarely in the path of the cavalcade of American military history.

During the French and Indian War, the North American component of the European Seven Years War, Pennsylvania lay between the English settlements along the Eastern seaboard and the French land claims along the Allegheny and Ohio Rivers (see map on page 4). Not even the formidable barrier of the Appalachian Mountains could keep the English colonists from encroaching on these river valleys that the French called theirs by right of exploration and commerce. Friction between the two sides inevitably sparked a fire that blazed into conflict, much of it taking place in western Pennsylvania. A strategic location like the forks of the Ohio in western Pennsylvania became a firepit. First the French built Fort Duquesne there to protect their interests; then the British conquered it and constructed their own Fort Pitt.

During the Revolutionary War, the rebel leaders proclaimed their independence from England in the colony's major city, Philadelphia. Then they sent out armies of citizen-soldiers to meet the veteran British troops. Many early battles between these farmers-turned-militiamen and the seasoned but overconfident redcoats occurred in Pennsylvania.

During the Civil War, that traumatic struggle born of basic differences in economies, cultures, and lifestyles between the North and South, Gettysburg, Pennsylvania, was the scene of the farthest advance of the Confederate forces into the North, an advance that was blunted and turned back by the Union victory. The park that preserves the landmarks of the largest battle ever fought on Pennsylvania soil is now the most visited Civil War national park in the nation.

Battles of four wars have been fought within the state's borders, in addition to several conflicts with indigenous Indians. In later years, when wars were fought far away in foreign lands, American men and women prepared and trained for combat at bases in Pennsylvania.

Some of these historic sites, such as Gettysburg, are preserved as national battlefields by the National Park Service, and some, such as Brandywine Battlefield, are maintained by the state. Others, such as the mansion at Cliveden, the vortex of the Revolutionary War Battle of Germantown, are kept open to the public by preservation organizations such as the National Trust for Historic Preservation. Still others, such as Fort Bedford, are proudly preserved by the town that grew up around it.

Many of us have family ties to these events, which link us to the country's history. We yearn to visit these memorial sites, to walk in the footsteps of our ancestors, to better understand why they fought. Reenactments of Revolutionary and Civil War battles each year draw thousands to watch the colorfully uniformed participants as they commemorate these historic events. The popularity of these reenactments testifies to our need to connect again with our roots.

Visiting a battle site provides new insights into history and its "what ifs." If the outcome of the French and Indian War had been different, Americans today might be speaking French instead of English. Walking the deck of the Brig *Niagara* in Erie brings to life the surprising fact that a major naval battle in the War of 1812 with Great Britain took place on a lake in the very heartland of our nation. And tiny Fort Necessity in western Pennsylvania was the site of a bitter defeat for twenty-two-year-old colonel George Washington.

History became very personal for us the day we visited Fort Pitt, a post commanded from 1781 to 1783 by Brig. Gen. William Irvine. The austere and somewhat forbidding General Irvine, we knew, was a direct ancestor of Marge's. At Fort Pitt, General Irvine was carrying out an order from General Washington to defend the western frontier during the Revolutionary War. Earlier, he had commanded troops during campaigns in New Jersey and New York. Much to our astonishment, we discovered that Molly Pitcher, the heroine of the Battle of Monmouth, had been a servant in the Carlisle household of General Irvine. She accompanied her husband to the battlefield and gained fame by stepping in to man a cannon battery when her husband was wounded. After the war, Irvine served in Congress. We crossed his path yet again while exploring the sites of the Whiskey Rebellion. It was General Irvine, we learned, who commanded the Pennsylvania militia that quelled this insurrection in western Pennsylvania. Seeing these events through his eyes revealed to us the past in a very personal way.

Walking where our forefathers fought taught us some essential lessons of history. So, too, may reading these pages give you new understanding of these actions that have woven themselves into Pennsylvania's history. Standing at the Bloody Angle at Gettysburg National Battlefield and visualizing the lines of Confederate soldiers advancing across that murderous open field may lead one to conclude that other ways than war must be found to resolve our deepest differences.

The weathered monuments and silent cannons we find at these

battle sites ask that we remember the crucial events that took place here and learn the lessons they teach.

HOW TO USE THIS BOOK

This guidebook is designed as a window on Pennsylvania's military past to help you discover the places where decisive actions took place that defined the destiny of this state and of the nation. In these pages, you may even find a site where your ancestors fought.

Some of these sites, such as Fort Mifflin and Cliveden, the site of the Battle of Germantown, still proudly preserve their original structures, little changed from the day that battle swirled around them. Others, such as Fort Ligonier and Fort Roberdeau, have been carefully restored to re-create the old fortifications. Still others commemorate the site with a monument, a museum, a restored ship, or a historical marker.

For an overview, look at the maps on pages xii–xvi, which pinpoint the locations of the thirty-eight historic military sites. Before starting out on a history tour or vacation trip, you might refer to these maps. That way, you may spot other military sites near the one you're going to visit and can plan your trip accordingly. Additional detailed directions in each section tell you the way to the site from the nearest major highways. For each site, the historical significance is described and useful visitor information is provided, including special events and nearby attractions.

We hope that this rich array of Pennsylvania's military history is as rewarding and exciting for you as it's been for us as we traveled the state gathering information from the people who know these sites the best. We're sure that you too will discover fascinating history around every turn in the road.

LOCATOR MAPS

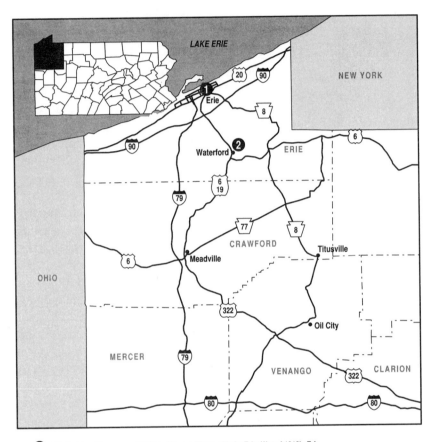

① Erie Maritime Museum and US Brig *Niagara* (Battle of Lake Erie, War of 1812), *Erie*

② Fort LeBoeuf Museum, *Waterford*

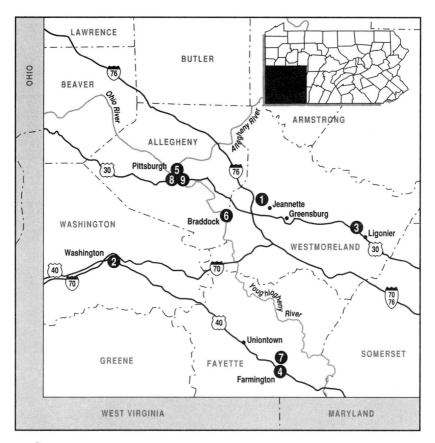

1. Bushy Run Battlefield (Pontiac's Rebellion), *Harrison City*
2. David Bradford House (Whiskey Rebellion), *Washington*
3. Fort Ligonier, *Ligonier*
4. Fort Necessity National Battlefield, *Farmington*
5. Fort Pitt Museum, *Pittsburgh*
6. French and Indian War Museum (Battle of Monongahela), *Braddock*
7. Jumonville Glen, *Farmington*
8. Soldiers and Sailors Memorial Hall, *Pittsburgh*
9. USS *Requin*, *Pittsburgh*

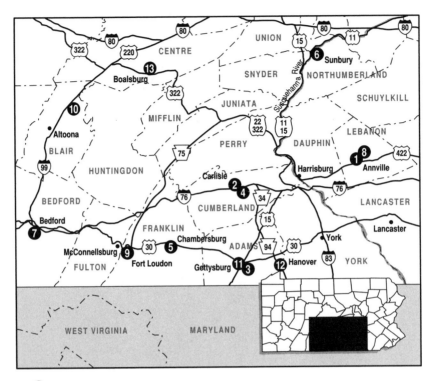

1. Battle of the Bulge Monument at Fort Indiantown Gap, *Annville*
2. Battle of the Bulge Monument at the U.S. Army War College, *Carlisle*
3. Camp Colt, *Gettysburg*
4. Carlisle Barracks, *Carlisle*
5. Chambersburg landmarks, *Chambersburg*
6. Fort Augusta, *Sunbury*
7. Fort Bedford, *Bedford*
8. Fort Indiantown Gap, *Annville*
9. Fort Loudoun, *Fort Loudon*
10. Fort Roberdeau, *Altoona*
11. Gettysburg National Military Park, *Gettysburg*
12. Hanover landmarks, *Hanover*
13. Pennsylvania Military Museum, *Boalsburg*

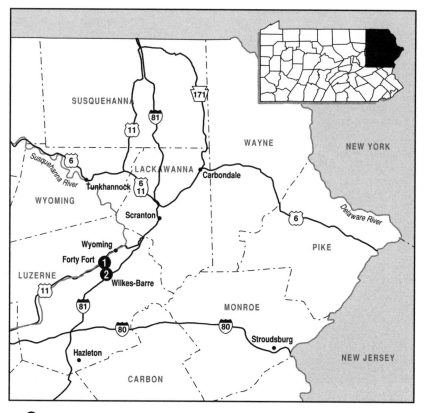

1 Wyoming Battle Monument (Battle of Wyoming Valley), *Forty Fort*

2 Wyoming Historical and Geological Society (Yankee-Pennamite Wars), *Wilkes-Barre*

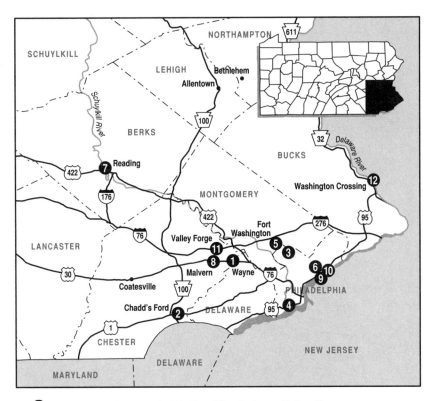

1. Battle of the Bulge Monument at the Valley Forge Military Academy and College, *Wayne*

2. Brandywine Battlefield, *Chadd's Ford*

3. Cliveden (Battle of Germantown), *Philadelphia*

4. Fort Mifflin, *Philadelphia*

5. Fort Washington State Park and Hope Lodge (Whitemarsh Skirmishes), *Fort Washington*

6. Independence National Historical Park, *Philadelphia*

7. Mid-Atlantic Air Museum, *Reading*

8. Paoli Memorial Grounds, *Malvern*

9. USS *Becuna, Philadelphia*

10. USS *Olympia, Philadelphia*

11. Valley Forge National Historical Park, *Valley Forge*

12. Washington Crossing Historic Park, *Washington Crossing*

LANDMARKS
OF THE
FRENCH
AND
INDIAN WAR

Fort LeBoeuf Museum

123 High Street
Waterford, PA 16444
814-732-2573
(at Edinboro University)

The French and Indian War was an outgrowth of the rivalry between France and Great Britain, as both countries sought to exploit the resources of the undeveloped lands of North America. A resource that quickly caught their eye was the lustrous pelts of the many animals that populated the continent. To opportunistic adventurers from Europe, the furs they procured from Indian trappers represented the path to commercial success. Fortunes awaited those who could fill the increasing demand back in Europe.

In the 1500s, French entrepreneurs developed an extensive fur trade with Indians living along the St. Lawrence River, around the Great Lakes, and in the heart of the country along the Ohio and Mississippi Rivers. French *voyageurs* paddled their canoes from dawn to dusk, packing enormous loads as they made their way along uncharted rivers and lakes. In their great birchbark canoes, some as long as 30 feet, they carried goods such as axes, pots, knives, trinkets, rum, and later, muskets, which they traded to the Indians in return for canoesful of furs.

In the 1600s, English settlers developed a thriving fur trade of their own along the Atlantic seaboard, extending their trading area from Maine to Georgia. Indian fur trappers or their middlemen, the Iroquois, brought their furs east to trading posts at Oswego on Lake Ontario or Albany on the Hudson River.

By the 1740s, French and British fur traders were competing bitterly over trading rights in the region where these two domains met—the area between the Allegheny Mountains and the Mississippi River. In 1749, French explorer Pierre Celeron de Bienville, while exploring the Allegheny and Ohio Rivers, buried lead plates at a number of locations, claiming the territory for France. The deep-seated rivalries that had already existed among the various tribes of Indians that had long lived in this area became intertwined with the newer rivalries of the Europeans. The Iroquois League, often known as the Five Nations, was a particularly influential and powerful group of Indians that occupied much of what is now New York State and dominated the fur-trading routes to both French Montreal and English Albany. The Iroquois

3

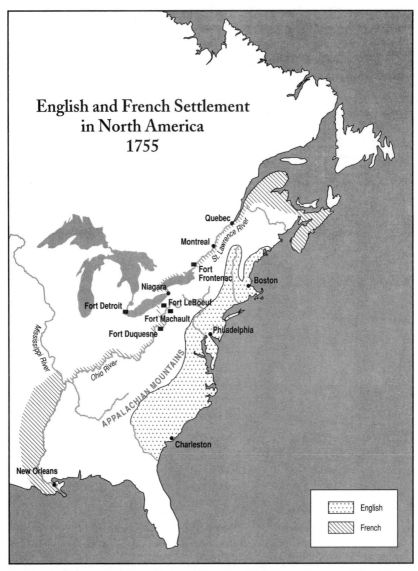

Rivalry between English settlers on the colonized East Coast and French traders along the Allegheny and Ohio Rivers ignited the French and Indian War in 1754.

tended to support the English against the French, but they often found advantage in playing one side against the other.

This commercial rivalry over the fur trade in North America became an extension of ongoing struggles that were being waged back in Europe among Great Britain, France, and other countries. Religious differences added yet another dimension to these tensions—almost all the French adventurers were Roman Catholic, whereas most of the English were Protestant.

In the 1750s, a spark ignited this smoldering rivalry. The Iroquois permitted a group of British colonists to settle in the Ohio River Valley, a region the Indians had previously forbidden to both the French and the British. The French feared that this would drive a wedge between their outposts on the Great Lakes and their colony at New Orleans and that they would lose the Ohio country's fur trade. To prevent this, they strengthened their claim to the area by building a chain of forts along the Allegheny River, the extension of the Ohio River into Pennsylvania. From the earliest days of French exploration of the river system that connects the Great Lakes with the Gulf of Mexico, trailblazers recognized that the forks of the Ohio, where the Monongahela and Allegheny Rivers meet to form the Ohio River, was a strategic location. It was a key site in an era when waterways provided the easiest means of moving from place to place. With their newly built forts, usually small stockades with garrisons of half a dozen men, they hoped to hold back the British colonists east of the Alleghenies.

The first of these forts, built under order of the Marquis de Duquesne, the governor of New France, was Fort Presque Isle on the shore of Lake Erie. A log stockade 120 feet square was completed in August 1753. A historical marker today identifies the site at Sixth Street and Parade Street within the city of Erie.

Some 15 miles south of Fort Presque Isle, the French built Fort de la Rivière aux Boeufs, or Fort LeBoeuf, in 1753. Fort LeBoeuf was situated on a tributary of French Creek at the first point that was deep enough for canoes. From here, the creek flowed southward to connect with the Allegheny River and thence with the Ohio and Mississippi Rivers. A portage path for canoes, first used by the Indians and later by the French, ran between Presque Isle and LeBoeuf. The portage took advantage of a unique geological feature, surmounting the escarpment left by the retreating glacier that had formed Lake Erie, then leading downslope to French Creek and the southward-flowing stream system. This was the only portage required for a journey by water from the Great Lakes all the way to New Orleans on the Gulf of Mexico.

The British, expanding their colonies on the eastern seaboard, watched with growing concern these French efforts to assert dominance over the Allegheny-Ohio River corridor. In 1753, just a short while after the completion of Fort LeBoeuf, the colony of Virginia took action. A group of Virginia investors called the Ohio Company had

Washington's Epic Wilderness Journey

An epic trek through the wilderness to Fort LeBoeuf in 1753 by Maj. George Washington was an early and risky exploit in his remarkable career. The ambitious twenty-one-year-old surveyor volunteered his services to Lt. Gov. Robert Dinwiddie of the Virginia colony. His mission: To deliver a strong official warning from England's King George II to France's military forces that they were intruding on the Ohio River Valley, which England claimed as her own. This assignment took him more than 1,000 miles through Indian country during the cold, wet winter of 1753–54. Scarcely four months later, the confrontational relations between the English traders and settlers and the French traders and soldiers in the river valley escalated into the French and Indian War.

The journey took Washington along rivers and through dense forests from Virginia to the small French fort located in the far northwest corner of Pennsylvania near Lake Erie, a trip he made on horseback, by canoe, on foot, and even by raft across an ice-choked river. He might never have succeeded in the hazardous venture without two men he persuaded to go with him—Jacob van Braam, a former lieutenant in the Dutch Army who acted as interpreter, and Christopher Gist, a frontiersman and woodsman who had experience dealing with the Indians. Washington also hired four wranglers to pack and tend the horses and set up camp.

Setting out from Wills Creek on November 15, the group crossed the rugged ridges of the Allegheny Mountains, then followed the Youghiogheny and Monongahela Rivers to the forks of the Ohio, the point where the Allegheny and Monongahela Rivers meet to form the Ohio River, the site of present-day Pittsburgh. Leaving the others for two days to reconnoiter, Washington carefully examined the area. This spot, he realized, would be a highly strategic location

negotiated an agreement with Indians of the Ohio River Valley that allowed them to trade in the area. To inform the French that the Virginians opposed the French claims to the valley, Gov. Robert Dinwiddie sent twenty-one-year-old George Washington on a long trek through the wilderness to warn the French to leave the country because Britain laid claim to both the Allegheny and Ohio River Valleys. The Virginians' assertion was denied and Washington was sent back empty-handed.

A replica of the map (with original spelling intact) that Washington presented to Gov. Robert Dinwiddie of Virginia upon his return to Williamsburg in January 1754. The original map, which demonstrated Washington's surveying skills, depicted his 1000-mile trek through the wilderness to present Dinwiddie's demands to the French at Fort LeBoeuf.

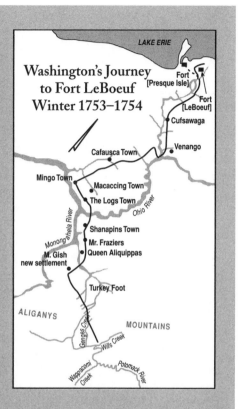

Washington's Journey to Fort LeBoeuf Winter 1753–1754

in any struggle to control the Ohio River system. He made sketches and took notes, which he later turned into a detailed report that strongly recommended building a fort at this location. Others apparently felt the same way, as it became the site of the French Fort Duquesne and later the English Fort Pitt.

The group forced the horses to swim across the Allegheny River, then proceeded downriver to the Indian town of Logstown, today's Ambridge, for an important meeting with Indians who were friendly to the English. Four Indians from the village agreed to accompany the expedition, guide them to the French fort, and hunt to provide meat for *continued on page 8*

The event, however, intensified the French-British competition for the valley.

Washington described the outpost in his journal: "Four houses compose the sides; the bastions are made of piles driven into the ground, standing more than twelve feet above it and sharp at the top, with port holes for the small arms to fire through. There are eight six-pound pieces in each bastion and one piece of four pounds before the gate. In the group. One who joined the party was an Oneida chief named Tanacharison, called Half King by the English. He had been humiliated by the French and intended to tell the Frenchmen that his tribes now renounced an agreement they had previously made with them.

After five days' travel northward in cold, snowy weather, along trails the Indians knew well, the group arrived at Fort Machault, an Indian village and French outpost at the juncture of the Allegheny River and French Creek (the site of today's Franklin). Here Washington met French frontier soldiers for the first time. The French were hospitable to the envoy, and at dinner the brandy flowed freely. The Frenchmen confirmed what the Virginians believed—that the French were determined to fortify the Ohio River and Mississippi River Valleys and to reinforce their claim of the entire water corridor for France.

The next day, the party pushed on toward Fort LeBoeuf (today's Waterford), where the ranking French commander was located. Through four more days of bad weather and miry conditions, they followed French Creek northward for 60 miles until they arrived at the fort, a rectangular enclosure almost surrounded by water.

These Frenchmen, too, treated the travelers hospitably. Washington met with the commandant, Legardeur de St. Pierre, and formally delivered his letter from Governor Dinwiddie stating that England claimed this river valley and calling on the French to vacate the region. Just as formally, St. Pierre delivered a written response to Washington disavowing this "pretension of the King of Great Britain" to the river valley. "As to the summons you sent me to retire, I do not think myself obliged to obey it."

Now came the tough part—making their way back through the frigid wilderness to Virginia. The horses were showing signs of weakness from lack of feed. Washington sent the wranglers and the horses on ahead, while he and the others took two canoes the French had given them and made their way by river. For six days and 130 miles,

the fort are a guard house, chapel, doctor's lodging and the commander's private store, round which are laid platforms for the cannon and men to stand on. There are several barracks without the fort for the soldiers' dwelling, covered some with bark and some with boards, made chiefly of logs."

Some 60 miles farther south, where French Creek flows into the Allegheny River, the French built their third fort, Fort Machault, at the site of an Iroquois Indian village, the location of present-day they paddled, chopped their way through freezing water, and dragged their canoes over rocky shoals, until they reached Fort Machault.

Half King wanted to rest here for a day or two, but Washington insisted on moving on, wanting to get word back to Dinwiddie as fast as he could. Leaving the Indians behind, the Virginians with their weakened horses headed down the trail. After three days of slow progress, Washington decided to leave the horses with van Braam and the wranglers, and he and Gist struck out alone on foot.

After escaping the gunfire of a treacherous Indian whom they had enlisted to guide them, the pair reached the Allegheny. The river was not frozen over as they had expected. They spent the next day building a raft, and the following morning they shoved it into the icy river and climbed aboard.

Partway across, they became jammed in the ice and had to abandon the raft. They swam to a nearby island, where they built a fire and huddled around it. By the next day, the channel between the island and the far shore had frozen solid. The two men walked across the ice and hiked to a trader's cabin, where they warmed themselves and found refuge.

On New Year's Day 1754, Washington set out on the final leg of his journey, now once more on horseback. He was cheered to meet a group of Virginians carrying materials to construct a fort at the forks of the Ohio. Some days later he came across "some families going out to settle" at the same site. Governor Dinwiddie was evidently not wasting any time solidifying the English claim to the Ohio River.

On January 16, one month and 500 miles after he had left Fort LeBoeuf, he rode into Williamsburg and handed the letter from St. Pierre to Governor Dinwiddie, miraculously intact. The reply erased any doubt that the French were determined to claim the entire Ohio-Mississippi waterway as their territory. It was clear that France and England were on a collision course in this valley in the New World. ∎

Franklin. When the French arrived, they drove out a Scotsman, John Frazer, who had set up a trading post among the Indians where he also repaired guns for the tribesmen. The French incorporated Frazer's cabin within the walls of the new fort that they completed in 1756.

Before the French could continue downriver and build the fort they desired at the strategic "forks of the Ohio," present-day Pittsburgh, the colonists from Virginia beat them to the punch. Governor Dinwiddie sent a detachment of men in 1754 to build a fortified structure at the forks to solidify Britain's claim to the area. One of the officers in charge of construction of what was called Fort Prince George was John Frazer, the gunsmith who had been ejected from his trading post at the site of Fort Machault.

The fort being built by the Virginians was never completed, however, because the French, angered at the Virginians, sent a force of 500 Frenchmen and Indian warriors to the forks, forcing the Virginia work crew to surrender the half-completed fort and return home. The French immediately began construction of their own fort at this vital location and named it Fort Duquesne.

The competing interests of the French and the British soon escalated into open conflict. In May 1754, Washington and a raiding party killed ten Frenchmen at Jumonville Glen. In July 1754, the French retaliated, defeating Washington at Fort Necessity. The following year, Maj. Gen. Edward Braddock, trying to capture Fort Duquesne, was routed and mortally wounded by the French and Indians at the Battle of Monongahela.

But the tide soon turned against the French as Maj. Gen. John Forbes built the Forbes Road from Carlisle across the wilderness and led another force against Fort Duquesne in 1758. With the fall of Duquesne, the French recognized that their forts to the north were vulnerable. As they retreated before the British, the French abandoned and set fire to Fort Machault, Fort LeBoeuf, and Fort Presque Isle, burning them to the ground.

In July 1760, Col. Henry Bouquet, who had superintended the building of the difficult Forbes Road to Fort Duquesne, led an army of 500 men northward to build a new British fort at both LeBoeuf and Presque Isle. Another, smaller detachment built a new Fort Venango at the site of the former Fort Machault.

Three years later, Fort LeBoeuf had to defend itself—not against the French, but against the Indians. Chief Pontiac had launched a coordinated attack on many of the British frontier forts. He called a war council in the spring of 1763 of all the northern tribes, and the Indians vowed to purify themselves by throwing off the white man's way of life and driving the English from their forts. Pontiac's Rebellion began in what are now Ohio, Michigan, and Indiana in May and soon thereafter swept into Pennsylvania.

On June 17, 1763, the little garrison at LeBoeuf was surrounded. All day the battle raged. Several times the attacking Indians set fire to the stockade, but the soldiers extinguished the blazes. With no reinforcements in sight and their water used up, the soldiers managed to escape. Hiding in a nearby swamp while the Indians burned the fort, they later made their way south to Fort Pitt.

The forts at Presque Isle and Venango were also captured and burned and their defenders either slain or taken captive. The Indians captured Venango by stealth. One story is that the Indians that heretofore had been friendly traders with the occupants of the fort appeared outside its gates for a game of lacrosse. One player deliberately threw the ball over the stockade wall. When an unsuspecting soldier opened the gate, the Indians stormed inside, slaughtering its defenders.

Three decades later, a third Fort LeBoeuf was built by the Americans, this time as a blockhouse surrounded by a stockade, to protect the growing town of Waterford from Indians. Projections jutting out from the second level of the blockhouse permitted riflemen to fire down at attackers from three different directions. All traces of this last fort disappeared by the mid-1800s.

WHAT YOU SEE TODAY

Fort LeBoeuf Museum. A modern building close to the location of the early fort offers a self-guided tour of exhibits relating to the history of the fort and the region. Displays describe the trade in beaver furs and explain the differences between the French and British methods of colonization. The Indian Room features a model of a palisaded Indian village. A slide show provides an explanation of George Washington's 1753 visit. A large, detailed model of the old fort is on display at the nearby Fort LeBoeuf Middle School. The museum is administered by the department of sociology, anthropology, and social work of Edinboro University of Pennsylvania for the Pennsylvania Historical and Museum Commission.

Statue of George Washington. In a small park across the street from the museum stands a statue of the twenty-one-year-old George Washington in the uniform of a major in the British militia. He is portrayed as he visited Fort LeBoeuf in 1753, handing the letter from the colony of Virginia to the French commander.

When to visit: Open most weekends throughout the year, noon to 4 P.M. Open for guided group tours by appointment. Call 814-732-2573.

Admission fees: Free.

Tours of the site: Self-guided.

Time needed to visit: One hour.
Special considerations: Handicapped accessible.
Parking: Free, in rear.
Directions: At 123 High Street, on PA Route 19, at the south edge of Waterford.

Other nearby sites

Judson House and Eagle Hotel. The Judson House is a restored Greek Revival home built in 1820 by Amos Judson, a trader who was one of the earliest settlers of Waterford. Visitors see many original pieces of furniture and implements, including a piano that was carefully transported over the Allegheny Mountains. Across the street stands the restored Eagle Hotel, a stagecoach inn built in 1826. The Fort LeBoeuf Historical Society operates both sites with the cooperation of the Pennsylvania Historical and Museum Commission.

Drake Well Museum. Located in Titusville, this site marks the spot where Col. Edwin Drake, in 1859, drilled the first commercially successful oil well in the United States. Exhibits, photographs, a video presentation, and outdoor field equipment, including a replica of the Drake well, tell the history of the Pennsylvania oil industry. A 10-mile paved bicycle trail and 30 miles of hiking trails connect the Drake Well and Oil Creek State Park. For information, call 814-827-2797.

Oil Creek and Titusville Railroad. A two-and-a-half-hour train ride in 1930s passenger cars that depart from Drake Well Museum. A tour guide and audiotape describe the history of the oil boom and the local scenery. The railroad station is located at 409 South Perry Street in Titusville. For reservatons and information, call 814-676-1733.

Fort Pitt Museum

Point State Park
101 Commonwealth Place
Pittsburgh, PA 15222
412-281-9285

By the 1740s and 1750s, the French and British were embroiled in territorial disputes that grew out of a rivalry over the fur trade in North America (see pages 3–11).

In 1754, Governor Dinwiddie sent a detachment of men to build a fortified structure at the forks of the Ohio to stake out a British claim, but the French forced the surrender of the fort and began to construct one of their own, naming it Fort Duquesne. Fort Duquesne remained the keystone of French operations in the Ohio River Valley for the next several years.

In 1755, the French inflicted a devastating defeat on Gen. Edward Braddock, who with his army of 2,000 had marched west to try to conquer Fort Duquesne. The next three years saw French-inspired hit-and-run attacks by Indians on the English frontier settlers, including vicious scalpings and murders. Enraged, the British in 1758 mounted another major effort to capture Fort Duquesne and push back the French. This time certain other factors favored the British. Back in Europe, France had become even more deeply involved in other dimensions of the Seven Years War, of which the French and Indian War was a part, and needed to send troops to other parts of the world. To meet this requirement, they pulled some of their forces out of North America.

Not only did the French in America reduce their regular troops, but they also lost some of their Indian allies at the same time. The eastern Delaware Indians, who had been forced from their lands along the Delaware River by European settlers, had moved to the Ohio River Valley, where they had become allies of the French. In October 1758, in a conference called by the peace-loving Quakers at Easton, the Colonial government of Pennsylvania heard the complaints of thirteen Indian nations, including the Delawares. As a result of the conference, Gov. William Denny of Pennsylvania promised the Indians that no settlement would occur west of the Allegheny Mountains. Thus reassured, the Delawares of Ohio turned to more peaceful ways. They changed their tribal leadership, substituting a peace chief, Tamaqua, for their war chief. Withdrawing their warriors from Fort Duquesne,

ROBERT GRIFFING

In the Shadow of the King *by Robert Griffing. The winter of 1763–64 was harsh. Wars and weather had taken their toll, forcing Indian families into the confines of Fort Pitt. Dependent on the British for their survival, the Indians found themselves living in the shadow of the King of England.*

they abandoned their support of the French and thus further weakened the fort's defenses.

The British moved on Fort Duquesne, this time with a large force of some 2,000 soldiers. But first they had to build a military road, the Forbes Road, to take them across the rugged mountains as they hauled their wagons and artillery.

Along the way they built supply forts—Fort Bedford and Fort Ligonier. This careful step-by-step campaign led by Gen. John Forbes was almost upset at the last moment by the rash actions of one of his subordinates. Maj. James Grant of the 1st Highland Regiment was ordered to take 850 men and make a reconnaissance of Fort Duquesne in preparation for a later all-out attack by the main force. But instead of restricting himself to reconnoitering, Grant attacked the fort. He was outmaneuvered, surrounded by 800 Frenchmen and Indians, and routed. The British lost 300 dead and wounded. When Major Grant was captured, the rest of his force retreated to Fort Ligonier.

But then Forbes got some good news. A spy brought word that Duquesne had been further weakened by the loss of its Indian allies. When Forbes's troops were only 10 miles away from Duquesne, scouts brought further word that the French had abandoned their fort in the face of the overwhelming odds that faced them. They blew up their powder magazine, burned the fort, and withdrew. The forks of the Ohio were now in British hands.

Construction was completed in 1761 on a new fort, this one named Fort Pitt in honor of Secretary of State William Pitt, who had authorized the mobilization of the forces that enabled Forbes to succeed. In the next few years, it became the most elaborate fort in English America. Except for sporadic attacks by marauding Indians, Fort Pitt came under serious attack only once. In 1763, a force of Indians taking part in Pontiac's Rebellion, an uprising of Indians against the British frontier outposts, maintained a siege on Fort Pitt for two months.

When the Indians besieging the fort got word that a British relief force was on its way from Fort Ligonier, however, most of them left Fort Pitt to confront the advancing British troops, who were under the command of Col. Henry Bouquet. The British force defeated the Indians at the Battle of Bushy Run. Following the battle, Bouquet's men made litters for their wounded, destroyed the supplies they could no longer carry because of their loss of horses, and marched on to Fort Pitt. There they found that the Indians had abandoned the siege.

Settlers in increasing numbers now pressed westward across the mountains, ignoring the provisions of earlier treaties. They clamored for protection against the Indians whose land they were taking. Ironically, it was the cost of the ongoing war with France as well as the increasing cost of defending these westward-moving settlers that drove Britain to assess the heavier taxes that eventually led to the American Revolution.

The last British troops to be assigned to Fort Pitt left it before the Revolution, in 1772. After the Revolution began, a patriot force under George Rogers Clark set out from Fort Pitt to occupy Vincennes, a trading post on the Wabash River in Indiana, and Kaskaskia, an island on the Mississippi River. Clark took both posts from the British, who had gained them earlier as a result of the defeat of the French.

During the Revolution, Fort Pitt became the headquarters of the Continental Army's Western Department. As such, it was the central coordinating point for responses to the Indian raids, which resumed in 1778 and continued until 1783. With the end of the war, Fort Pitt became one of two storage depots, along with West Point, for the army's military supplies and equipment.

By the time Fort Pitt was abandoned in 1792, the frontier had been won, and the town of Pittsburgh, which had grown up around the fort, boomed with merchants and traders. Many of them made their living provisioning the flatboats and the wagons of settlers who were pushing even farther west, past the forks of the Ohio.

WHAT YOU SEE TODAY

Geographically, little has changed at the confluence of the three rivers over the past three centuries, but the city of Pittsburgh, physically the second largest in Pennsylvania, now surrounds the historic site. You have to search hard for the last remnant of Fort Pitt—a brick blockhouse, built under orders of Colonel Bouquet to provide covering fire over the moat that surrounded the fort. Of the five blockhouses built to strengthen the fort in 1764, this is the only one that remains. It's one of the oldest structures west of Carlisle and the oldest building in Pittsburgh. The historic structure provides a sharp contrast to the sleek skyscrapers and elevated expressways nearby. Several bronze plaques near the blockhouse commemorate the construction of the Forbes Road and of the blockhouse.

Today a reconstruction of one bastion of the star-shaped fort houses the Fort Pitt Museum, which offers an array of dioramas, relief maps, artifact exhibits, period rooms, uniformed models, and paintings. Its exhibits depict not only the historic events associated with Fort Pitt, but

This blockhouse built in 1764 is the only original structure remaining from Fort Pitt, once the strongest fort in the American colonies. A contemporary museum nearby contains exhibits that reflect how soldiers lived at the frontier outpost.

also the evolution of Pittsburgh as an Indian trading post, a frontier settlement, an early transportation hub, an industrial metropolis, and an intellectual and cultural center. When a major renovation of the museum is completed, the facility will offer new exhibits, an art gallery, interactive video displays, workshops, and a research library.

The highlight of Fort Pitt's educational program is a re-created regimental unit, the 60th Royal Americans of Foot, which portrays the daily lives of soldiers at the fort in a series of programs throughout the year. The group is also involved in the annual Fort Pitt Assembly, a reenactment of life at Fort Pitt during the time of its occupation. Troops from several units encamp at the park, providing demonstrations of camp life, military drill, and artillery practice. The assembly culminates with an eighteenth-century costume ball.

When to visit: Wednesday through Saturday; 10 A.M. to 4:30 P.M.; Sunday, 12 noon to 4:30 P.M. Museum closed on certain holidays.

Admission fees: Adults $4, children $2, seniors and groups $3.50, family $10.

Special events: Fort Pitt Assembly, occasional living-history encampments, and musket-firing demonstrations.

Tours of the site: Self-guided.

Time needed to visit: Two hours.

Special considerations: Handicapped accessible.

Parking: Commercial parking nearby.

Gift shop: Books, booklets, videos, postcards, and memorabilia.

Directions: Fort Pitt Museum is in Point State Park, which lies at the tip of Pittsburgh's "Golden Triangle." From the east, approach on I-376; turn right on Stanwix Street, then left on Boulevard of the Allies; turn right on Commonwealth Street to park entrance on left. From the south, approach on I-279, then cross Fort Pitt Bridge, and continue on Liberty Avenue; turn left on Commonwealth Street to park entrance.

Tourist information

Greater Pittsburgh Convention and Visitors Bureau, 4 Gateway Center, Pittsburgh, PA 15219, telephone 800-366-0093, fax 412-644-5512, website www.pittsburgh-cvb.org.

Other nearby sites

Senator John Heinz Pittsburgh Regional History Center. This museum and research facility devoted to the history and heritage of western Pennsylvania contains a varied collection of glass, antique furnishings, portraits, and documents, as well as Discovery Place for children. Located at 12 Smallman Street near the University of Pittsburgh and the Carnegie complex of libraries and museums in Oakland. Open daily. For information, call 412-454-6000.

Old Economy Village. Located in nearby Ambridge, the site of the original town of Economy, this village was built between 1824 and 1830 by the Harmony Society, a Christian communal society. The community prospered in agriculture, textile manufacturing, and other industries. The 6.5-acre restored village contains seventeen original structures. Closed Mondays. For information, call 724-266-4500.

Rivers of Steel Heritage Area. One of nine state-designated heritage regions, this area includes sites that tell the history of industrial barons and the toil of thousands of immigrants. In 1875, a blast of fiery heat from a new Bessemer in Braddock began the age of steel. By 1900, Carnegie Steel had employed 20,000 people. Learn more about the rivers and people that made it possible. For information, call 412-464-4020.

Jumonville Glen

Fort Necessity National Battlefield
1 Washington Parkway
Farmington, PA 15437
724-329-5512

A skirmish in the forests of southwestern Pennsylvania in 1754 was
the spark that brought to a flashpoint the smoldering rivalry in
North America between two aggressive colonial powers—France and
England (see pages 3–11).

When Washington returned from his long trek to Fort LeBoeuf (see
pages 6–9), Governor Dinwiddie sent him off on another mission.
He and a detachment of militiamen were to support the Virginia workmen who were building a fort at the forks of the Ohio. But before Washington, now a full colonel, could reach the construction site, a superior
force of French troops had forced the Virginians to leave. The French
then built a fort of their own at the same site, which they named Fort
Duquesne.

The work party retreated to Virginia, but Washington and his contingent continued to move onward, intending to determine the extent
of French penetration into the region. By late May, they had reached
Great Meadows, a large, natural clearing some 60 miles from the forks.
Washington decided to make this his base camp, as the meadow had
grass and water for the horses.

Soon after he arrived, he received word from a friendly Indian
chief, Half King, that a contingent of French soldiers was camped in a
ravine several miles away. On the stormy night of May 27, 1754, Washington and about forty men began an all-night march to confront the
French and learn their intentions. They traveled through woods so
dark that the men sometimes spent nearly half an hour just trying to
find the trail.

About dawn, Washington met with Half King, who had scouted the
French camp. The French commander had not posted sentries, and
Washington and his men easily surrounded the unsuspecting French.
Someone fired a shot and soon the peaceful glen was filled with the
sounds of musket fire and the sulphurous smell of gunpowder. The battle
lasted about fifteen minutes. When it ended, ten Frenchmen were dead,
including the leader of the group, Ens. Joseph Coulon de Villiers, Sieur
de Jumonville. The Colonials captured twenty-one men, although one

escaped and made it back to Fort Duquesne with word of the engagement. One of Washington's men was killed and two or three wounded.

Washington realized that he had been discovered and the French would soon be seeking retribution. After sending his prisoners under guard to Williamsburg, he returned to Great Meadows. Immediately he began constructing a small fortification to protect his force from an attack he was now sure was coming.

WHAT YOU SEE TODAY

Today the glen where musket shots rang out two and a half centuries ago is a quiet spot. A gravel road leads the visitor to a grassy clearing in the dense forest. A bronze plaque set in a rough-textured rock announces that here Washington and his band of Virginians, "assisted by the Half King, Tanacharison, and a company of Indians surprised, killed, wounded or captured the entire engaged French force under the command of Ensign Coulon de Jumonville." Under this explanation is historian Francis Parkinson's evaluation of this seemingly minor skirmish on the American frontier: "This obscure skirmish began the war that set the world afire."

Down a trail that descends around a rocky precipice, there is a flat area where the French were undoubtedly camped, an easy target for the Colonial militiamen firing down on them from atop the rocks.

When to visit: Open daily, April 15 to October 31, 10 A.M. to 5 P.M.
Admission fees: Free.
Tours of the site: Self-guided.
Time needed to visit: Half an hour.
Parking: Free.
Directions: See Fort Necessity National Battlefield directions (page 24). Then go 3 miles from visitors center to flashing traffic light and turn right. Follow road and direction signs for 2 miles to Jumonville Glen.

Other nearby sites
See Fort Necessity National Battlefield (pages 22–23).

Fort Necessity
National Battlefield

1 Washington Parkway
Farmington, PA 15437
724-329-5512
fax: 724-329-3682
website: www.nps.gov/fone

After the engagement at Jumonville, Washington took his troops back to their base camp at Great Meadows, where they quickly erected a frontier fort for protection against the retaliatory attack they were sure was coming. Washington called it a "fort of necessity." They built a circular stockade 53 feet in diameter, upending logs in a narrow trench to form a barricade and hewing the top end of each log into a point. Inside the stockade, they constructed a small storehouse to hold guns, powder, and supplies. They dug a trench in front of the small fort, using the dirt to build an earthwork that would offer some protection to the soldiers lying behind it.

Reinforcements arrived at Fort Necessity on June 9, 1754, along with supplies and nine swivel guns. With his augmented forces now numbering about 400, Washington and his men continued to fell trees and create the rough roadway they had been working on, which he hoped would one day lead a future British army across the mountains to conquer Fort Duquesne.

By the end of June, 600 French troops and militia, accompanied by 100 American Indians, were on their way from Fort Duquesne. Commanding the force was Capt. Louis Coulon de Villiers de Jumonville, half brother of the commander the British had killed only a month before. As soon as they got word of the approach of the French force, the British, working on the road 13 miles west of Great Meadows, retreated to defend their hastily built fort.

On July 3, the French struck. British attempts to lure the enemy out into the open failed, and a siege began in a steady rain. The British defenders in the trenches had to lie in puddles of water, while the French could fire easily at the Colonials from their hidden positions behind the trees in the surrounding forest. By sunset, the British, who had numbered 400, had suffered thirty dead and seventy wounded. The

Visitors today can see the small, crude stockade that Washington called a "fort of necessity." The palisades of the reconstructed fort are set into the exact location of the original postholes as determined by archeologists.

fighting continued sporadically until about 8 P.M., when the French commander called for a truce to discuss surrender terms.

Washington, fearing the French would make a bayonet charge with their Indians wielding tomahawks, was willing to talk. About midnight, after several hours of negotiation, the terms were put in writing, and the document was signed by Washington and his co-commander. The British were allowed to surrender with the honors of war, retaining their baggage and weapons, but having to give up their swivel guns. They further agreed that British forces would stay east of the Appalachian Mountains for the next year, and they left behind two men as hostages to guarantee that the French prisoners they had taken at Jumonville would be returned. Then they marched out with the full honors of war and returned to Virginia. The French burned Fort Necessity and marched back victoriously to Fort Duquesne.

WHAT YOU SEE TODAY

The stage is still set at Fort Necessity, much as it was two and a half centuries ago when Col. George Washington, then a British officer, tried to defend this small stockade from a numerically superior force of French and Indian attackers. In 1953, the National Park Service did a thorough archaeological investigation of the site and unearthed twelve original post fragments and numerous musket balls, as well as buttons, flints for muskets, clay pipestems, and a bolt that was probably from an old wagon.

A path from the visitors center leads you across the Great Meadow to the surprisingly small stockade. A British Colonial flag flies from the flagpole during the summer. The reconstructed fort occupies the site of the original fort, and the palisades are in the exact location of the original stockade posts. The trenches in front of the fort are reconstructions of those strengthened by Washington's men between their return to the fort on July 1, 1754, and the beginning of the French attack on July 3.

During summer months, a ranger dressed as either a British or French Colonial militiaman gives talks to visitors about life as a soldier of the time. Other programs relate to the role of American Indians, including an interpreter playing the role of an Indian who was fighting on the side of the French.

The Braddock Road Trace, which runs past the fort, is a remnant of the road built by Washington's troops in 1754 and improved by General Braddock's men on their way toward Fort Duquesne the following year. Today visitors may walk on a series of interconnecting loop trails that wind through mixed deciduous forest and stands of pine.

The park also preserves and interprets a reminder of a later time in American history, 1828–1855, when this same location became a busy stagecoach and wagon stop, serviced by the Good Intent Stagecoach Line. The stagecoaches rumbled by on the newly constructed National Road, the first highway built by the federal government. The Mount Washington Tavern, one of the largest early structures on this portion of the National Road, was a welcome sight to travelers, offering lodging, meals, news, and refreshments. George Washington purchased the land on which the tavern was built in 1769 and owned it until his death in 1799. The tavern now contains period furnishings in several of its rooms. A Conestoga wagon, the workhorse vehicle of those days, is on display in a shed next to the tavern.

When to visit: Open daily from 8 A.M. to sunset. The visitors center is open 9 A.M. to 5 P.M. year-round, except Thanksgiving, Christmas, and New Year's Day.

Admission fees: Adults $2, children 16 and under free.

Special events: July 3: memorial program; weekends in July and August: encampments. Also, musket firings, Indian displays. Check park's website www.nps.gov/fone, for current calendar of events.

Tours of the site: Mid-June to mid-August. Ten-minute slide show at the visitors center.

Time needed to visit: Two hours.

Special considerations: Handicapped-accessible restrooms; use of wheelchair available.

Parking: Free.

Gift shop: Books, booklets, postcards, and videos.

Directions: On U.S. Route 40, 11 miles east of Uniontown, Fayette County.

Other nearby sites

Ohiopyle State Park. The 14-mile Youghiogheny River Gorge cuts through this 19,046-acre gateway to the Laurel Mountains, providing some of the best whitewater rafting in the East. The park offers camping and picnicking, as well as 41 miles of hiking and biking trails, including the southern terminus of the 70-mile Laurel Highlands Trail.

Laurel Caverns. Pennsylvania's largest cave, with 2.8 miles of passages; the caverns are formed of limestone and feature catacombs and intricate sculpting. Open seven days a week from May 1 to October 31, with guided one-hour tours. Caverns Park Road is located off U.S. Route 40 east of Uniontown.

National Road Heritage Region. One of nine state heritage regions, developed around the history of a 90-mile segment of U.S. Route 40, National Road Heritage Region tells the story of American growth, development, migration, and the historic towns and sites along the route. Headquarters are at 3543 National Road in Farmington, telephone 412-329-1560.

French and Indian War Museum

BATTLE OF THE MONONGAHELA

First Carnegie Library
419 Library Avenue
Braddock, PA 15104
412-351-5358
fax: 412-351-6810
e-mail: beckerm@clpgh.org

By 1755, the French were winning the contest for dominance in the Ohio River Valley. Their string of forts—Presque Isle, LeBoeuf, Machault—along the Allegheny River system, anchored by Fort Duquesne, had successfully held the British at bay. They had defeated Washington at Fort Necessity. Their Indian allies were harassing and killing settlers who had moved into central and western Pennsylvania and frightening other settlers into giving up and going back east.

But the British refused to give up. They were ready to undertake the difficult task of moving an armed force through the Appalachian Mountains to mount an attack against the French strongpoint at Fort Duquesne.

A thousand crack infantrymen and nineteen artillery pieces were sent from England to the colonies and were joined by Colonial troops. After augmenting the force with the Colonial militiamen and a few Indians, it numbered 2,400 men, though not all of them took part in the forthcoming battle. It was the most potent military force that North America had yet seen. It was led by Maj. Gen. Edward Braddock, at age sixty a career soldier who had risen through the ranks with forty-five years of service. He was commander in chief of all British forces in North America. This veteran soldier had little respect for his French and Indian opponents. "These savages," he once told Benjamin Franklin, "may be a formidable enemy to raw American militia but upon the King's regulars and disciplined troops they can make no impression."

The overall British plan for 1755 was to simultaneously attack several French forts in North America. Braddock himself would lead the expedition against Fort Duquesne. George Washington, then twenty-three years old, signed on as a volunteer aide to the general. In June, this military force left its training ground at Fort Cumberland in Maryland on the Potomac River and began the arduous 110-mile march that would bring it to the forks of the Ohio. A large corps of men was sent ahead of the main body for the strenuous task of chopping a road through the immense forest. Braddock had even conscripted thirty sailors to assist in dragging the heavy artillery over the mountain ridges. Only eight Indians, however, remained from a much larger original contingent, to serve as scouts through the forest.

After a full month of backbreaking progress, the advance party had hacked a 12-foot-wide path, later known as Braddock's Road, to the banks of the Monongahela River and had forded the river to come within 20 miles of Fort Duquesne.

Meanwhile, the French were getting regular reports from their Indian scouts on the progress of the redcoats. Though the French and their Indian allies had only about two-thirds as many soldiers as the British—most of them Indians—they possessed a superior strategy. Rather than wait for the formidable British force with its cannons to lay siege to Fort Duquesne, the French commander, Capt. Claude Pierre Pecaudy, also known as Contrecoeur, decided to surprise the attackers in the forest, where the town of Braddock now stands. As the column of redcoats marched smartly up the newly cleared roadway, French soldiers and Indian warriors, taking cover behind trees to protect themselves, attacked from both sides with a murderous cross fire. Smoke filled the ravine, and many British officers fell early in the battle, leaving their troops leaderless.

George Washington in British Colonial uniform stands atop a monument that marks the site of the Battle of Monongahela in the borough of North Braddock. The French and Indian War Museum nearby displays artifacts of the 1755 battle. This same field was used nearly forty years later for a mass protest during the Whiskey Rebellion.

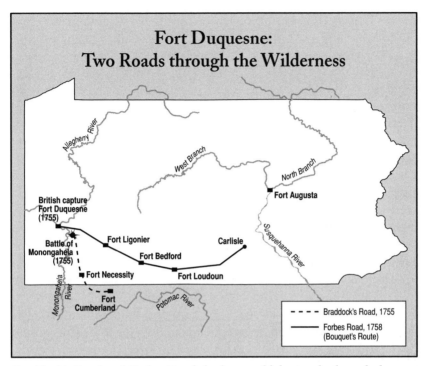

Braddock's Road and Forbes Road, both carved laboriously through the mountainous wilderness of western Pennsylvania, shared the same destination—the forks of the Ohio River.

As British troops from the rear rushed up as reinforcements, they ran into others streaming back from the front. The British column collapsed into a mass of frightened men. The shocked troops ignored their officers' orders and bunched together under the withering fire, too fearful to either flee or move against the enemy. Braddock himself was in the thick of the battle. After having four horses shot out from under him, he was hit in the lungs and was carried, mortally wounded, from the field.

The British suffered nearly 1,000 casualties out of 1,300 combatants in three hours of fighting an enemy who found shelter behind trees and occupied a commanding hill. The officers at the rear abandoned their artillery pieces and supplies. Especially damaging was the loss of Braddock's written battle plans, which gave the French details of the British blueprint for attacking other French forts.

The French lost only a handful of men. They apparently had instructed their Indian allies to concentrate their fire on the British officers, for sixty-three out of eighty British officers were killed. Washington had two horses shot out from under him. He later found four bullet holes in his uniform, but amazingly, he was not injured.

The British survivors, thoroughly disheartened, retreated back toward Cumberland, 100 miles to the rear. It was a humiliating defeat for General Braddock and the British forces. On the way back, the wounded Braddock, who had been carried carefully by his men for four days, finally died. The troops buried him near the site of the former Fort Necessity, which had been burned to the ground only the year before. To prevent the Indians from discovering the gravesite and dishonoring his remains, Washington ordered the soldiers to bury Braddock's body in the roadway and to disguise the site by driving wagons back and forth across it. His body was later reinterred nearby and a monument erected.

WHAT YOU SEE TODAY

Braddock's Field. A statue of George Washington marks the site of the battle in the borough of North Braddock, 10 miles east of the Point in Pittsburgh. Now a school recreation field, the site is on Jones Avenue, two blocks north of Braddock Avenue.

French and Indian War Museum and Gallery. Located in the First Carnegie Library at 419 Library Street in Braddock. Visitors may view artifacts of the battle, including belt buckles, cannonballs, and spontoon blades; many of these items were unearthed by archaeologists at the nearby battle site. Historical maps and prints of scenes from the Braddock expedition by Robert Griffing and other artists encircle the room.

When to visit: Monday through Friday, 9 A.M. to 6 P.M.; Saturday, 9 A.M. to 4 P.M.

Admission fees: Free; donations appreciated.

Tour of the sites: Self-guided with a printed tour guide.

Time needed to visit: One hour.

Special considerations: Located on second floor, but handicapped accessible.

Parking: On street.

Directions: Take exit 11 from Pennsylvania Turnpike to Forest Hills, turn right on Yost Boulevard, turn left on Braddock Avenue, and left again on Library Street to the museum.

Other nearby sites

Braddock's Grave. A 12-foot-high granite monument rests in a grassy park at a pull-off along U.S. Route 40, 1 mile west of Fort Neces-

A 12-foot-high granite monument stands at the site where Gen. Edward Braddock died during the British retreat after the ill-fated Battle of Monongahela. The monument is located 1 mile west of Fort Necessity, where Washington had suffered a defeat thirteen months earlier.

sity National Battlefield. After the battle on July 9, 1755, which took place 50 miles northwest of the monument site, the British retreated with their mortally wounded general. Braddock died on the evening of July 13. Washington officiated at the funeral ceremony the next day. "He [Braddock] was interred with the honors of war," Washington later wrote, "and as it was left to [me] to see this performed, and to mark the spot for the reception of his remains—to guard against a savage triumph, if the place should be discovered—they were deposited in the road over which the army wagons etc. passed to hide any trace by which the entombment could be discovered."

From the monument, a path leads through a swale that identifies the location of the original military road. A hundred yards down the path stands a simple marker that identifies the actual spot in the roadway where the British general was buried. In 1804, some workmen discovered human remains at this spot. The remains were removed and reinterred a short distance away at the monument site. The imposing monument was erected by the Braddock Park Memorial Association in 1913.

See also Fort Pitt Museum and Fort Necessity National Battlefield.

Fort Bedford Museum

Fort Bedford Drive
Bedford, PA 15522
814-623-8891 or 800-259-4284
e-mail: fbm@nb.net
website: www.nb.net/~fbm

Braddock's unexpected defeat by French and American Indian forces at the Monongahela River in 1755 left the Pennsylvania frontier vulnerable to Indian attack. The Shawnee and Delaware tribes now had the chance for revenge they had been waiting for. Encouraged by the French, the Indians began to attack the settlers all along the frontier as they took revenge for the loss of their former lands. As a result, many settlers abandoned their homes in the wilderness and fled back east. Hundreds of others were killed before they could get away, and many women and children were taken as tribal captives.

To protect the colony, a chain of forts was built all along the frontier, from Easton on the Delaware River west to the Allegheny Mountains. The Pennsylvania Colonial government built a number of small forts and manned them with militiamen. Between 1756 and 1763, some 200 settlers fortified their own homes and farms against possible Indian attack.

The colonists pleaded for more military help from the mother country. When William Pitt became secretary of state of Great Britain in 1757, these pleas fit into Pitt's own strategy of trying to oust the French from the Ohio Valley. Pitt agreed to send over a large army of professional soldiers from England, and the colonists agreed to furnish supplies and to raise their own militias. Pennsylvania's Assembly, no longer controlled by Quakers, who opposed armed conflict, voted money for the war and took steps to enlist some 3,000 volunteers.

Pitt ordered a second expedition to conquer Fort Duquesne, built by the French at the forks of the Ohio, the point where the Allegheny and Monongahela Rivers meet to form the Ohio River, the site of today's city of Pittsburgh.

To lead this Royal American Regiment, British authorities hired soldiers of fortune from other European countries. In America, many German settlers of Pennsylvania and Maryland were recruited into the regiment. One of these European mercenaries was Henry Bouquet, a Swiss army officer who was appointed a colonel and second in command to British general John Forbes, who headed the strike force.

Faced with a wilderness crossed only by Indian paths, Bouquet directed the building of what became known as the Forbes Road, which allowed the expedition to pull its wagons westward over the Allegheny Mountains. Along this line of supply and communications from Carlisle to the Ohio River, he supervised the building of a chain of forts. Constructing this 100-mile-long roadway was a huge task, and it had to be completed in one season to make it possible for Forbes's army to subdue Fort Duquesne before winter brought a halt to all operations.

The route followed a path known to the Indians and to traders. It surmounted one mountain ridge after another as it pushed across the Alleghenies. The men felled hundreds of trees, shoveled earth to make the roadway, and built bridges across creeks. Today's U.S. Route 30, the Lincoln Highway, closely follows the Forbes Road from Bedford to Pittsburgh. At Rohr's Gap, west of Bedford, you can still see traces of the original military road that was hacked out of the wilderness two and a half centuries ago.

At the road's midpoint, Forbes's men built Fort Bedford in 1758. Strategically located on a bluff overlooking the Juniata River, Fort Bedford controlled the river gap and served as a stockade for the supply of the vanguard of men advancing over the mountains to Fort Ligonier and Fort Duquesne. Encompassing an area of 7,000 square yards, the fort had five bastions, places for swivel guns to guard the corners of the irregularly shaped stockade.

The stockade was built by digging a ditch, 4 or 5 feet deep, outlining the area. Logs 18 feet in length were flattened on two sides, upended in the ditch, and fitted closely together. They were fastened securely near the top, and the upper end of each log was hewn to a point. A number of platforms were erected within the stockade for riflemen to stand on with loopholes cut in the stockade wall at frequent intervals for the riflemen to fire through. Portholes were cut into the corner bastions to allow for the firing of the swivel guns. Finally, a moat was dug along two sides of the fort.

A novel feature of the fort was a protected, covered passageway that led from the fort down to the river. Soldiers could walk along the passageway to get water, safe from arrows or rifle shots.

WHAT YOU SEE TODAY

Fort Bedford existed until the 1770s, when it deteriorated and disappeared, and archaeologists have found no trace. The Fort Bedford Museum is housed in a blockhouse-style structure reminiscent of the original fort. It holds an impressive, large-scale model of the fort and depicts the Forbes Road and the surrounding terrain. Thousands of items of the frontier days are displayed, including a well-preserved flag given to the fort by England's Lord Bedford, for whom the fort and town were named, as well as flintlock rifles, a cannonball from the fort, clothing of the period, antique hand tools, household items, and Indian arrowheads and spearpoints.

When to visit: Open daily May through October, except Tuesdays, 10 A.M. to 5 P.M. April, November, and December, weekends only.
Admission fees: Adults $3, seniors $2.50, children $1.50.
Tours of the site: Call for information.
Time needed to visit: One hour.
Parking: Free.
Gift shop: Books, pamphlets, maps, and souvenirs.
Directions: Take exit 11 off the Pennsylvania Turnpike. Turn right on Business Route 220. Travel south 2 miles. At second traffic light, turn right on Pitt Street. Turn right at next traffic light onto Juliana Street. Museum is on your right.

Tourist information
    Bedford County Visitors Bureau, 141 South Juliana Street, Bedford, PA 15522, telephone 800-765-3331 or 814-623-1771, website www.bedfordcounty.net.

Other nearby sites
    Old Bedford Village. Located 2 miles from Fort Bedford, just outside the town of Bedford. Here you step into the days of the frontier settler. More than forty structures have been relocated here from other locations in Bedford County and preserved for the public, including early log homes, a two-story 1762 farmhouse, two schoolhouses, a church, craft shops, a working Colonial farm, a tavern, and a covered bridge. Knowledgeable guides greet you at the various buildings. A broommaker, potter, tinsmith, blacksmith, storekeeper, quiltmaker, baker, candlemaker, cobbler, farmer, weaver, doctor, tanner, and brewer demonstrate their skills. May 1 through August 31, open daily except Wednesday, 9 A.M. to 5 P.M.; September and October, open Thursday through Sunday, 10 A.M. to 4 P.M. There is an admission fee, and shops sell Colonial craftwork. For more information, call 814-623-1156 or 800-238-4347.
    David Espy House. See David Bradford House (Whiskey Rebellion), page 123.

National House. Recently restored as the Golden Eagle Inn at 131 East Pitt Street (originally the Forbes Road), this 1790 brick building was once owned by Dr. John Anderson, who opened the Golden Eagle Tavern on the ground floor of his mansion to serve stagecoach passengers and traders going to market. The tavern also provided food and shelter for George Washington's troops during the Whiskey Rebellion. The National House Antique Gallery occupies the space of the original tavern. Today, the inn serves lunch and dinner and offers sixteen guest rooms and suites. Telephone 814-623-9020.

Bedford County Covered Bridges. A 90-minute driving tour of fourteen century-old bridges begins at Old Bedford Village. Pick up a tour map at the visitors center.

Pioneer Historical Society of Bedford County. Contains genealogical files and family histories, U.S. censuses, and cemetery records of Bedford County.

Lincoln Highway Heritage Corridor. One of nine state heritage regions, this 140-mile segment of U.S. Route 30 is known as the Lincoln Highway. The corridor extends through Westmoreland, Somerset, Bedford, Fulton, and Franklin Counties. This east-west route was once a well-used Indian pathway, then the Forbes Road was built along it to Fort Ligonier and Fort Pitt. Later it was transformed into a busy stagecoach route, then a turnpike linking Philadelphia and Pittsburgh, and in the age of the automobile, it became the start of America's first transcontinental highway. *Lincoln Highway Driving Guide* and *Lincoln Highway Journal* are available free from the Lincoln Highway Heritage Corridor, P.O. Box 386, Greensburg, PA 15601, 724-837-9750.

Fort Ligonier

216 South Market Street
Ligonier, PA 15658
724-238-9701
fax: 724-238-9732
e-mail: ftlig@westol.com
website: www.ligonier.com/fortligonier.html

The years 1755 to 1758 marked the high point of France's bid for supremacy in the Ohio River Valley. The French strategy was to establish a string of forts from Lake Erie southward, along the natural pathway of the Allegheny River and the Ohio River, then down the Mississippi River, where their forces could link up with the French settlement in New Orleans. By thus erecting a sort of "fence" of fortifications, they hoped to contain the expansion of British and other European settlers who were pushing westward over the Allegheny Mountains from their settlements along the East Coast.

Fort Duquesne, at the forks of the Ohio, was to be the key link in this line of fortifications. The French built their fort there in 1754, at the same site where only a year before they had driven away a band of Virginians intent on doing the same thing for the British. After the French and their Indian allies triumphed over Braddock's expedition in 1755 (see pages 25–28), they enjoyed complete control of the Ohio River Valley.

This French supremacy in America angered her longtime enemy, Great Britain. When William Pitt became secretary of state, he commissioned a powerful force under a veteran military officer, Col. John Forbes, to subdue Fort Duquesne and thereby drive a wedge in the French line of forts (see pages 30–31).

After the army built Fort Bedford, it followed a traditional Indian pathway westward. Army engineers constructed a roadway across the rugged western Pennsylvania terrain, completing the 50 miles in thirty days as far as Loyalhanna Creek, the eventual site of Fort Ligonier. In fashioning this route, General Forbes ignored Colonel Washington's urgent plea that he follow the existing route taken earlier by Braddock, which led from Fort Cumberland on the Potomac River toward Duquesne. Although the Forbes route had to be hacked out of the forest wilderness; it was some 40 miles shorter than the Braddock route, it avoided several river crossings, and the countryside provided good forage for the expedition's animals.

Loyalhanna had formerly been the site of a Delaware Indian village. Forbes ordered a fortified camp to be built here as a staging area for his final assault on Fort Duquesne. Col. James Burd and an advance party of about 1,500 men began construction of the fort in September 1758. Its design was basically a square, 200 feet on a side, with bastions protruding at each corner, surrounded by a large outer retrenchment. It was named in honor of British field marshal Sir John Ligonier, commander in chief of the British Army.

Construction had hardly been completed when a French force attacked. Forbes and the main body of troops had not yet reached the fort, and Col. Henry Bouquet, his second in command, was away. Colonel Burd was in charge at the fort. The defenders withstood a four-hour attack. After nightfall, the French and Indians attacked again but were driven back by mortar fire from the fort. The British lost sixty-three men killed, wounded, and missing, and the French suffered losses as well. They "were employed all night carrying off their dead and wounded," Burd reported. This was enough to discourage the French, who retreated back to Fort Duquesne.

Forbes and the rest of the army finally arrived at Ligonier in early November, seemingly too late in the season to mount an attack on Duquesne. Forbes was very ill and had been carried for miles on a litter slung between two horses. Luck was with them, however. Prisoners who had been captured during another skirmish confessed that the defense force at Duquesne was now severely weakened. Not only had the commander of Duquesne lost a number of men in the fruitless attack on Ligonier, but he had also been ordered to send some of his soldiers to reinforce French forts to the north, and most of his Indian allies had returned to their villages.

Learning this, Forbes decided to mount the attack on Fort Duquesne immediately, rather than wait for spring, when the weather would be better. Faced with this challenge, the army succeeded in clearing the final 56 miles of the Forbes Road from Ligonier to Duquesne in only twelve days.

On November 24, only a few miles from their objective, the weather turned bad. Some of the officers advised returning to Ligonier, but during the night, scouts reported seeing a cloud of smoke rising above Fort Duquesne. Soon afterward, word arrived that the fort had been torched and abandoned by the French. The next day, Forbes saw for himself that the fort was almost entirely destroyed, along with thirty nearby houses. The French had given up in the face of the superior British force. Forbes had captured his objective without firing a shot, taking possession of this key strongpoint in the Ohio River Valley. He renamed the site Fort Pitt.

WHAT YOU SEE TODAY

Fort Ligonier has been reconstructed in authentic detail to give the impression of entering an actual eighteenth-century frontier fort. With its palisaded outer walls, dry moat, inner fort with corner bastions, fascine batteries, and the log buildings within, it vividly re-creates the old stronghold. To make the scene even more realistic, life-size figures in period dress portray the activities that took place here: soldiers withdrawing stores from the commissary, officers relaxing in their quarters, the doctor treating a patient. Visitors may also climb down to inspect the underground powder magazine.

Fort Ligonier is the most thoroughly researched and reconstructed French and Indian War fort in Pennsylvania. Archaeological investigation unearthed 100,000 articles, which now bring history to life for visitors.

Just outside the fort stands a replica of the hut the soldiers built for their ailing commander, Gen. John Forbes. Even though he was ill at the time, Forbes accepted command of the expedition. He mapped the overall strategy for the campaign, but he left much of the day-to-day operations to his deputy, Col. Henry Bouquet. Forbes showed great courage in withstanding the grueling march from Carlisle to Duquesne. He died in Philadelphia just four months after his great victory at Duquesne.

The results of archaeological digs at the site are displayed in a well-designed museum outside the reconstructed fort. More than 100,000 artifacts have been unearthed, the richest lode from any French and Indian War site in the United States. Among the items on display are glass bottles, a cowbell, iron spikes, pieces of a soldier's canteen, the leather sole of a soldier's shoe, and surprisingly, even an apple that was preserved by the cool silt of Loyalhanna Creek.

A short film acquaints the visitor with the global reach of the Seven Years War between France and England and describes the U.S. part of this conflict, known as the French and Indian War. Dioramas portray the Forbes Road and Fort Duquesne. Another wing of the museum houses changing exhibits and displays of decorative arts, weapons, and other items relating to the military and cultural life of the period.

When to visit: Open April through October 31, Monday through Saturday, 10 A.M. to 4:30 P.M.; Sunday 12 noon to 4:30 P.M.
Admission fees: Adults $6, seniors $5, children $3.
Special events: A weekend in September: Ligonier Highland Games; second weekend in October: Fort Ligonier Days.
Tours of the site: Self-guided.
Time needed to visit: One and a half hours.
Special considerations: Handicapped accessible.
Parking: Free.
Gift shop: Books, booklets, gifts, and souvenirs.
Directions: Fort Ligonier is located 50 miles east of Pittsburgh in the town of Ligonier on U.S. Route 30 and PA Route 711. Use Pennsylvania Turnpike exit 9.

Tourist information

Laurel Highlands Visitors Bureau, 120 East Main Street, Ligonier, PA 15658, telephone 724-238-5661, website www.laurelhighlands.org. Publishes the *Laurel Highlands Visitors Guide,* a guide to the region of Fayette, Somerset, and Westmoreland Counties, and provides brochures on local travel destinations.

Other nearby sites

Compass Inn Museum. A restored stagecoach stop in Laughlintown, 4 miles east on U.S. Route 30, the restored inn has a working kitchen, blacksmith shop, and barn, and is furnished with period pieces. The log section was built in 1799 and the stone addition in 1820. Living-history events on weekends during the summer, and candlelight tours on weekends in November and December.

Lincoln Highway Heritage Corridor. See page 33.

Fort Augusta

Northumberland County Historical Society
1150 North Front Street
Sunbury, PA 17801
717-286-4083

The resounding July 1755 defeat of Gen. Edward Braddock's British force by the French-led Indian fighters at the Battle of the Monongahela (see pages 25–29) left dozens of settlements and homesteads west of the Susquehanna River vulnerable to attacks by marauding Indians.

A number of colonists had settled farther westward, beyond the grants of land that had been purchased legitimately from the Indians by proprietors Thomas and Richard Penn. These settlers had simply occupied good farmland they found in the Susquehanna River Valley. There they built their cabins, tilled the land, and raised their families.

Meanwhile, the remainder of Braddock's army, which had marched so confidently toward Fort Duquesne and had been defeated, now retreated to the protection of Fort Cumberland, many miles to the south on the Potomac River, far from most of the frontier settlements.

Braddock's defeat and death had redoubled the resolve of the French authorities in the Ohio River Valley to push back the English settlers east of the Allegheny Mountains. The French had long considered the Alleghenies to be the natural boundary for English settlement along the East Coast. But the French had few soldiers to mount a sustained attack against the frontier settlers and their militias. Instead, they incited their Indian allies to harass, raid, burn, torture, and kill.

It was the Delaware and Shawnee who led these raids. Both tribes had previously been forced from their traditional homelands along the Delaware River by the influx of white settlers. Now they had established new villages to the west along the Ohio River. They were angry with the Iroquois, allies of the British and the dominant Indian tribe in the Northeast, because the Iroquois had sold land the Delaware and Shawnee considered to be theirs. Consequently, they allied themselves with the French in opposition to the westward expansion of the English settlers.

The government of the colony of Pennsylvania, dominated by Quakers, who traditionally sought peaceful solutions to controversies, tried to intervene diplomatically between the settlers and the Indians.

38

The attempt failed. Finally, Pennsylvania governor Robert Morris reluctantly declared war on the Delaware and Shawnee Indians.

By October 1755, as the settlers were threatened by the French and Indian war parties, the fear that was such a familiar part of frontier life was spreading east and south across the Allegheny Mountains. Without British armies, and with few Colonial troops (mainly George Washington's Virginia regiment) brave enough to search the forests for the Indians, the settlers were forced to either flee to the east or turn their log homes into fortified blockhouses.

The native warfare was characterized by small numbers, swiftness, mobility, and destruction and was harrowing to soldiers and civilians alike. French-led parties of Indians would strike suddenly at dawn, burning houses, butchering horses and cattle, and frequently killing and scalping or, if possible, dragging away men, women, and children to be adopted into the tribe to replenish its dwindling population.

Settlers in the Susquehanna River Valley became terrified after the Penn's Creek Massacre of October 16, 1755, the first in a wave of killings by Indians. Jean Jacques Leroy had built a cabin for his family along Penn's Creek, a western tributary of the Susquehanna, upriver from present-day Harrisburg. According to his daughters, who witnessed the tragedy and survived, eight Indians appeared and killed their father as he tried to defend his family. They carried the girls off as captives. Twenty-five other inhabitants of Penn's Creek also were killed or taken prisoner. Penn's Creek typified the Indian raids, in which war parties attacked unsuspecting farm families, mutilated their murdered bodies, and looted and destroyed their farms.

Similar frightful slaughters took place all along the British border in Virginia, Maryland, and Pennsylvania. Hostile Indians swarmed eastward, using the rivers as highways, and plundered both west and east of the Susquehanna. As a result, Colonial settlers fled.

Rumors circulated that the French, taking advantage of the evacuation of the region by the British, would build a fort at the forks of the Susquehanna, where the northern and western branches of the river meet. Years later, the French admitted they had indeed planned to build a fort at the site but turned back when they discovered that a large number of British soldiers were already at work there constructing a fort.

The settlers who remained in the area cried for help to defend themselves. Even the friendly Iroquois, allies of the British, asked Pennsylvania governor Morris to build a fort at Shamokin, an Indian village at the forks of the Susquehanna. In response to such calls for action, and to forestall any French move into the area, the Pennsylvania legislature in 1756 called for the construction of a line of forts along the frontier.

Back in England, the government realized that the French were pushing the English settlers eastward and gaining control of the Ohio River Valley. When William Pitt became secretary of state, he ordered renewed efforts to repel the French and regain control of western Pennsylvania and, hence, the important trade route of the Ohio River.

In April 1756, Governor Morris ordered Col. William Clapham and a regiment of 400 men to march up the Susquehanna to Shamokin and build a fort there. Clapham first built a supply fort, Fort Halifax, halfway between Harris's Ferry (now Harrisburg) and Shamokin (present-day Sunbury). He then loaded twenty boats with materials and poled them upstream to the forks of the Susquehanna while the main body of troops marched to the site.

The result was Fort Augusta, one of the largest and strongest of the chain of British frontier forts. The fort, named for the mother of King George III, was about 200 feet square, built of logs that were erected upright in the part facing the river and laid lengthwise to form the rear wall. The main wall of the fort was faced, or revetted, to about half its height by a dry ditch, or moat. A triangular bastion at each corner allowed for cross fire that could cover the entire wall. The fort mounted sixteen cannons, two of which are in the museum today. Inside the fort were officers' quarters and soldiers' barracks, a powder magazine, and a well. As many as 1,000 men were stationed at Fort Augusta. It was further protected by stockades stretching out from either side of the fort to the river. Along each stockade stood two blockhouses, forming a covered pathway to the river. This same protective feature was later used in the construction of Fort Bedford. A year later, an underground powder magazine was added, when the Colonial defenders realized they needed to store kegs of black powder safely so that a spark would not ignite a disastrous explosion.

Fort Augusta was never captured, besieged, or threatened by Indians, although one of the other forts in the frontier chain, Fort Granville, on the Juniata River, was besieged by a band of French-led Delaware Indians in July 1756. The flaming arrows fired by the Indians burned a gap in that fort's stockade. Now vulnerable to attack, Fort Granville surrendered.

In retaliation, Pennsylvania colonel John Armstrong, whose brother had been killed at Fort Granville, raised a force at another of the nearby forts, Fort Shirley. With 300 men, he marched west to the Allegheny River to Kittanning, the largest of the Indian towns in western Pennsylvania and the home of Delaware chief Captain Jacobs. In a sharp battle, Armstrong's men surprised the community of perhaps 100 warriors and a few French soldiers. Although Armstrong's men suffered heavy losses, they killed Captain Jacobs and a number of his warriors and burned the village. As a result, the Indians abandoned Kittanning.

By 1758, Britain had sent strong reinforcements to the colonies to quell the Indians. The Forbes offensive conquered Fort Duquesne, British control moved westward, and Fort Augusta was no longer on the frontier. In 1763, Pontiac's Rebellion, the Indian uprising, swept eastward from Detroit but failed to reach the Susquehanna. Fort Augusta served as a supply fort, providing men and matèriel to other forts in the effort to put down the rebellion.

Fort Augusta and the forks of the Susquehanna played one last role in the French and Indian War. Soldiers who had served with Col. Henry Bouquet in Ohio, where they ended Pontiac's Rebellion, were rewarded with grants of land near Fort Augusta.

In 1769, Gov. John Penn granted 24,000 acres near the forks of the Susquehanna to officers of the Pennsylvania Regiment of Foot. The largest tract was awarded to the commanding officer of the regiment, Col. Turbutt Francis. Andrew Straub, an early settler, later bought the land and in 1791 laid out the plan for the nearby town of Milton.

During the American Revolution, Fort Augusta served as the military headquarters of the American forces in the upper Susquehanna Valley. The activities of the Northumberland County militia, the mobilization of locals to serve in Washington's army, and the support and protection of smaller posts throughout the valley were directed from the fort by Col. Samuel Hunter, the county's chief military officer and one of the original builders of Fort Augusta.

WHAT YOU SEE TODAY

Powder Magazine. The powder magazine, which was built below ground in one of the bastions, and the well are the sole remnants of this once-strong frontier fort along the Susquehanna. Residential homes have been built where the fortifications once stood, and the terrain has been relandscaped. The well-restored brick magazine has thick walls and an arched roof.

Hunter House. Hunter House stands on the site of the commandant's quarters within the walls of Fort Augusta. When the original log house burned to the ground in 1848, the colonel's grandson, Capt. Samuel Hunter, built the present two-story brick Colonial-style dwelling. It now serves as a museum, displaying a variety of artifacts

Hunter House stands on the site where the commandant's log house once stood within Fort Augusta. Today it holds a museum and serves as headquarters for the Northumberland County Historical Society.

unearthed during six excavations at the site, including weapons, tools, utensils, household items, military decorations, Indian beads, and arrowheads, as well as two original cannons used at the fort. Upstairs is a historical and genealogical library. Behind Hunter House is a small, walled cemetery that holds the graves of Col. Samuel Hunter and family members.

When to visit: Open Monday, Wednesday, Friday, and Saturday year-round, 1 P.M. to 4 P.M.

Admission fees: Free; donations accepted.

Tours of the site: During open hours or by appointment.

Time needed to visit: One hour.

Special considerations: First floor and restrooms handicapped accessible.

Parking: Free.

Gift shop: Books, booklets, postcards, and memorabilia.

Directions: From U.S. Route 11 along the Susquehanna River, cross the river on PA Route 147 to Sunbury. Turn left on Front Street, and proceed to Hunter House, which faces the river.

Tourist information
Susquehanna Valley Visitors Bureau, RR 3, 219D Hafer Road, Lewisburg, PA 17837, telephone 570-524-7234 or 800-525-7320, fax 570-524-7282, website www.svvb.com. Serves Northumberland, Snyder, and Union Counties from its center at Hafer Road and U.S. Route 15, 2 miles north of Lewisburg, 5 miles south of I-80.

Other nearby sites
Shikellamy State Park. This park along the Susquehanna River encompasses 131 acres in Union and Northumberland Counties. The park was named for Chief Shikellamy, friend of the white settlers in eighteenth-century Pennsylvania. Activities include hiking, bicycling, picnicking, boating, and fishing.

Governor Snyder Mansion. Built in 1816, this was the Selinsgrove home of three-term Pennsylvania governor, Simon Snyder. During the Civil War, it was a station on the Underground Railroad and had a 350-foot tunnel that linked the house with the Susquehanna River bank to enable slaves to escape. It now houses a retail gift shop and brewery.

Joseph Priestley House. The Northumberland home of the "father of modern chemistry" and the discoverer of oxygen; Priestley lived here from 1794 until his death in 1804. Also a theologian, educator, and political philosopher, he came from England seeking a political and religious haven. The home, chapel, and visitors center offer exhibits and displays of his scientific accomplishments.

Slifer House Museum. The Victorian home of Col. Eli Slifer, secretary of Pennsylvania during the Civil War, the house was later a doctor's office, the original Evangelical Hospital, and a home for senior citizens. The museum schedules year-round events, including Civil War encampments, summer concerts, Victorian teas, and a Christmas soirée. Slifer House is located at 1 River Road, on the grounds of River-Woods, owned by Albright Care Services in Lewisburg.

Packwood House Museum. This three-story building, which grew from a small cabin built in the late 1790s, now houses more than 10,000 items of eighteenth-, nineteenth-, and twentieth-century furniture and art objects. Located at 15 North Water Street in Lewisburg.

Fort Loudoun

Fort Loudoun Historical Society
North Brooklyn Road
Fort Loudon, PA 17224
717-369-3318

The defeat of Braddock's overconfident army in 1755 and the withdrawal of the remainder of the British regular forces to Fort Cumberland on the Potomac River left the scattered settlers of the Pennsylvania frontier vulnerable to Indian attack. Without the British army to offer protection, and with few Colonial militiamen ready to prevent Indian attacks, the settlers were forced to either flee back east or turn their log homes into fortified houses.

Indian raids reached a peak between January and September 1756, when marauding bands of Delaware and Shawnee from the Ohio Valley roamed central Pennsylvania, killing settlers and burning their crops and homes. The Indian war parties even destroyed some of the fortified houses, called local forts, and defeated a sizable militia force in a pitched battle at Sideling Hill.

In another attack, Indians succeeded in conquering one of the colony's frontier forts, Fort Granville, located near present-day Mifflintown. The Indians shot fire arrows at the fort, burning an opening in the stockade. When the garrison, faced with imminent defeat, sought to surrender, the Indians killed the defenders.

Even a retaliatory raid led by Col. John Armstrong in September 1756 seemed to have little effect. Armstrong mobilized a force of 300 Pennsylvania militiamen and marched to the Indian town of Kittanning on the Susquehanna River, the largest Indian village in the colony. The militiamen routed the Indian warriors, burned the town to the ground, and dispersed its inhabitants.

Pennsylvania governor Robert Morris, who had heretofore tried to negotiate with the Indians, reluctantly declared war on the Delaware and Shawnee. He called for construction of additional forts in a line roughly following the contour of the Allegheny Mountains diagonally across Pennsylvania.

The newly constructed frontier forts gave the settlers more of a sense of security. The Indians, they knew, would usually refrain from assaulting a solid, well-defended fort unless they were commanded by French officers. On the other hand, they routinely overpowered individual settlers' homes, even when the armed settlers tried to defend them. Patrols of militiamen moved back and forth between forts, keeping an eye out for threatening Indan war parties in the area.

One of these frontier forts was Fort Loudoun, a stockade constructed to the east of the Tuscarora range of the Alleghenies near the Tuscarora Trail, a north-south Indian pathway. It was built in 1756 under the direction of Col. John Armstrong, the militia commander who led the successful campaign that destroyed Kittanning. The fort was built over and around a house and barn owned by Matthew Patton, whose farm had been attacked and burned the year before by the Indians.

To construct the fort, the militiamen dug a roughly square trench 127 feet on a side, with the corners angled or blunt rather than right-angled. In the 3-foot-deep trench, they set 18-foot-long logs, upright side by side, with smaller backup posts about 3 inches in diameter. At two corners inside the enclosure, they built shooting platforms supported by posts. An entrance gate was located on the north wall. Two structures, both with stone cellars, stood within the fort. A stone-lined well within the enclosure provided water for the troops of the garrison.

A view of the interior of Fort Loudon through a loophole in the stockade that permitted riflemen to fire at attackers. At the rear is one of the fort's two shooting platforms.

The fort was named for the Scotsman John Campbell, earl of Loudoun, who had just become the commander of all British forces in North America. Interestingly, another frontier fort, built the same year in Winchester, Virginia, was also named Fort Loudoun.

Few of the frontier forts possessed cannons, but many had swivel guns. These were weapons of a caliber greater than that of muskets but smaller than cannon barrels. They were mounted on a semicircular metal piece bolted into the sides of the barrel and had a pin extending straight downward that fit into an opening on the top of the stockade wall. Turning on the pin, the weapon could be swung horizontally in a 360-degree arc and fully elevated or depressed. Thus, accuracy did not depend on the gunner's ability to hold the weapon steady with his arms and absorb the recoil of the discharge against his shoulder, as it did with muskets and rifles. In defending against an attack, soldiers would fire a swivel gun from one of the corner platforms, while other riflemen fired at the enemy at ground level through loopholes in the stockade.

There seems to have been little variation from one frontier fort to another in terms of living conditions during the French and Indian War period. Life was harsh and grim, an endurance contest that left its mark on many a soldier. Diaries and official reports are filled with accounts of scarce or spoiled supplies, overwork, fatigue, disease, boredom, scarcity of female companionship, snakebites, excessive punishment, torture, chiggers, poison ivy, drabness, extremes of temperature, desertion, and personality clashes.

Fort Loudoun played an important role as a fortified supply depot during the Forbes Expedition of 1758. It also served as a meeting place for discussions with American Indians from the South who were being wooed by the British to join the fight against the French and their allies. It was a communication link along the Forbes Road during Col. Henry Bouquet's 1763 expedition, during Pontiac's Rebellion, and in 1764 when Bouquet marched to the Muskingum River Valley in Ohio to sign a peace treaty with the warring Indians.

The fort was also the scene of an unusual confrontation. In 1763, James Smith, a local resident, who had once been kidnapped and adopted by Indians for five years, was deputized by the farmers in the area to prevent unscrupulous traders from supplying unfriendly Indians with weapons and arms that could be used against the settlers. Smith formed a company of 300 rangers, who destroyed several pack trains suspected of carrying weapons and ammunition. When the traders fled to the protection of Fort Loudoun, Smith's Rangers fired on the fort for two days and nights, preventing anyone from leaving. Eventually, on November 11, 1763, the British garrison surrendered their arms and vacated the fort. Smith later became a colonel during the Revolutionary War.

On November 17, 1765, Gen. Thomas Gage ordered the garrison at Fort Loudoun to evacuate, thus ending the fort's nine years of service to Pennsylvania.

WHAT YOU SEE TODAY

In 1968, the Commonwealth of Pennsylvania purchased the original grant of land owned by farmer Matthew Patton. Today, the fort has been reconstructed as a state historic site west of Chambersburg near the Maryland border, just off U.S. Route 30 between Chambersburg and Breezewood. The site is preserved by the Pennsylvania Historical and Museum Commission and administered by the Fort Loudoun Historical Society.

Visitors today see an authoritative reconstruction of old Fort Loudoun, a stockade rebuilt on the basis of several archaeological investigations that determined its location and features. A 1977 excavation revealed the location of the palisade walls. A 1980–82 excavation disclosed a stone-lined well and remains of other structures, such as a barracks, midden, and root cellars. Hundreds of artifacts of prehistoric Indians who lived nearby were also unearthed. The visitor today, however, sees no visible signs of the buildings that once existed within the fort or of the well.

Archaeologists also unearthed evidence of the house that a farmer, Matthew Patton, had built at the location, finding the house's foundation and charred remnants of the structure, which was burned to the ground by Indians in 1755. They also turned up wine bottles, utensils, a pipe, a mouth harp, and other artifacts. An oaken bucket that had been submerged in the well water for two centuries was remarkably well preserved and is now on display at the State Museum in Harrisburg.

The visitors center for Fort Loudoun is a restored 1798 house originally erected at the site after the fort was abandoned. In its Log Room, visitors can examine the interior side walls showing the large logs used in its construction.

When to visit: Call to make an appointment.
Admission fees: Free.
Special events: Last weekend in June: Frontier Days, including reenactments that portray garrison life at the fort; November: French and Indian War Experience; December: Colonial Christmas at Fort Loudoun.

Tours of the site: Self-guided, or for appointment, write or call Mrs. Anna Rotz, President, Fort Loudon Historical Society, P.O. Box 181, Fort Loudon, PA 17224, 717-369-3318.
Time needed to visit: One hour.
Parking: Free.
Directions: Drive 14 miles west of Chambersburg on U.S. Route 30, and turn at the sign onto North Brooklyn Road.

Other nearby sites

Buchanan's Birthplace Historical State Park. Commemorates Stony Batter, the birthplace of James Buchanan, fifteenth U.S. president and the only one born in Pennsylvania (1791). As a young man, Buchanan practiced law in Lancaster, where he built his 1828 Federal mansion, Wheatland. He then served ten years in the House of Representatives, ten years in the Senate, and four years as secretary of state under James K. Polk before his term as president (1857–1861). The Park is located near Cove Gap on PA Route 16.

McConnellsburg. The town of McConnellsburg, nestled between the Tuscarora and Scrub Ridge Mountains along U.S. Route 30 (the Lincoln Highway), was founded in the 1760s by Daniel McConnell, who built a private fort to protect his family from warring Indians and later built a log house. The house still stands on the northwest corner of Lincoln Way and First Street. By the nineteenth century, McConnellsburg was a drivers' layover and stagecoach stop for travelers between Philadelphia, Pittsburgh, Baltimore, and Washington. Fulton House, once a major hotel, today serves as a local history museum and town hall.

Cowans Gap State Park. Named for Maj. Samuel Cowan, a British soldier who fell in love with the daughter of a Boston merchant during the Revolutionary War. Cowan's future father-in-law, opposed to the British, forbade him to see his daughter, forcing Cowan to return to England alone. But he couldn't forget his American sweetheart, so he returned to Boston and they eloped. The couple later headed west, but their rickety wagon made it only to the next county, where they traded it to an Indian chief in exchange for the land known as Cowans Gap. Built in the 1930s, the stone and log cabins are on the National Register of Historic Places. Fishing and a swimming beach are available at a 42-acre lake and the 1.5 mile Lakeside Trail is part of 10 miles of hiking trails.

LANDMARKS
OF THE
REVOLUTIONARY
WAR

Independence National Historical Park

313 Walnut Street
Philadelphia, PA 19106
215-597-8974
website: www.nps.gov/inde

Philadelphia, the largest city in the colonies, proved to be the hub around which much of the Revolutionary War swirled. It was here that the colonists found a common cause, opposing the repressive measures leveled on them by Great Britain. And it was here that opposition grew into action, when Americans took up arms to determine their own political destiny.

Over the eighteen years following the French and Indian War, when British soldiers and American militiamen pushed the French out of the Mississippi and Ohio River Valleys and claimed most of North America for Great Britain, controversy had increased between the colonists and their mother country. The American colonists had been largely self-governing for a century and a half, determining their own lives in a land they had converted from a wilderness into a home. Britain, on the other hand, felt it had received little financial help from the colonists in defeating the French. The French and Indian War had cost Britain dearly in both money and manpower. Now, with a greatly expanded colony, it needed additional revenue from those who stood to benefit the most: the American colonists.

To increase the cash flow, Britain levied a series of duties or taxes on goods that Americans imported. Some of the more outspoken colonists protested that this was "taxation without representation." The phrase became a rallying cry against the harsh economic measures imposed by the British.

When the British government ordered its troops to enforce the collection of these duties in Massachusetts, other colonies came to the support of the New Englanders. When angry Bostonians threw overboard bales of English tea in protest against yet another tax, other colonies also boycotted the imported tea and passed resolutions condemning the British administration. At the suggestion of Virginia, Colonial representatives were summoned to meet in Philadelphia on

51

September 5, 1774, "to consult upon the present unhappy state of the Colonies."

The delegates to this First Continental Congress sent a Declaration of Rights and Grievances to the king of England. The delegates conceded that Britain had the authority to regulate Colonial imports and exports, but they sought relief from the more restrictive of the recently imposed Coercive Acts.

Most of the delegates intended to remain part of the British Empire; only a few radicals advocated full independence. But King George III refused to compromise. "The Colonies," he said, "must either submit or triumph."

In April 1775, British troops stationed in Boston were ordered to confiscate gunpowder and military stores that were being stockpiled by colonists in nearby Concord. On the way, the redcoats were blocked by a band of fifty armed Minutemen at Lexington. A firefight ensued, and eight Americans were killed. This was the "shot heard 'round the world"—the first blood of the war for independence had been shed.

The events at Lexington and Concord galvanized the colonists. One month later, delegates from all thirteen colonies met in Philadelphia for the Second Continental Congress. They voted to raise an army and appointed Col. George Washington as its commander in chief. They adopted the Declaration of Independence, which called on the colonists to break away from Great Britain and unite as an independent nation. The document not only announced the birth of a new nation, but also set forth a philosophy of human freedom that would henceforth become a dynamic force in the entire western world. It rested not upon particular grievances, but upon a broad base of individual liberties that would command general support throughout America.

On the battlefield, the Continental Army at first suffered a series of defeats at the hands of the professional British soldiers, retreating from New York and across New Jersey. Other losses followed at Brandywine, Paoli, and Germantown. On September 26, 1777, the capital, Philadelphia, fell. Only farther north did the Colonial army meet with success. In October 1777, forces under Maj. Gen. Horatio Gates defeated a British force under Maj. Gen. John Burgoyne, who surrendered at Saratoga, New York. The victory at Saratoga, as well as a near victory by Washington's troops at Germantown, persuaded France to come to the aid of the Americans against their traditional foe. The French Alliance, which bolstered the spirits of the colonists, was announced seven months later during the Valley Forge encampment.

Meanwhile, Philadelphia was occupied by the British Army until June 1778. Congress fled to York, Colonial munitions were moved to Reading, the Liberty Bell was sent to Allentown, and Philadelphia merchants sent their goods out of town for safekeeping. British Maj. Gen. William Howe spent the winter comfortably in Philadelphia while his army camped at Germantown. General Washington and his soldiers barely survived on the cold and windswept slopes of Valley Forge.

WHAT YOU SEE TODAY

Independence National Historical Park Visitor Center. Park rangers guide visitors and provide materials that identify the historic sites, most of which are within a few blocks. A film sets the scene and gives an orientation to the park. The Bicentennial Bell, a gift from the people of Great Britain in 1976, hangs in the 130-foot bell tower. Information is also available for sightseeing in Philadelphia.

Carpenters' Hall. Meeting place of the First Continental Congress in 1774. It was built by the Carpenters' Company, a craftsmen's guild. During the Revolutionary War, the building was used as a military hospital by both the Americans and the British. It is still owned and operated by the Carpenters' Company.

Independence Hall. Centerpiece of the park, the hall was built between 1732 and 1756 as a governmental complex for the province of Pennsylvania. In 1753, a tower was added in which was hung the State House Bell, later called the Liberty Bell. Originally

The focal point of the Revolutionary War, Independence Hall was the scene of the adoption of the Declaration of Independence by the colonies in 1775 and of the appointment of George Washington to command the rebelling army. Congress was forced to flee the hall for York when the British captured Philadelphia in 1777.

called the State House, the hall was the scene of the Second Continental Congress in May 1775. It was at Independence Hall in June 1775 that George Washington was appointed commander in chief of the Continental Army. Here, too, on July 2, 1776, Congress passed a resolution that the colonies henceforth were independent of Great Britain, a resolution that was elaborated on in the Declaration of Independence, which was approved by the delegates on July 4. Except for brief absences due to military threats and the period of British occupation from September 1777 to June 1778, Congress continued to meet in Independence Hall until June 26, 1783. Independence Hall was also the location of the Constitutional Convention of 1787, when the federal Constitution was drafted and approved for ratification by the states. This Constitution, for the first time, blended the thirteen colonies into one nation with a federal government, a single currency, and one national military force.

Second Bank of the United States. Portraits of more than 180 of the political, military, and cultural leaders of the Revolutionary era are exhibited in this Greek Revival structure. Built in 1824, it was the successor to the First Bank of the United States as the center of federal banking.

New Hall Military Museum. Originally a new hall for the Carpenters' Company in 1791, it was reconstructed in 1957. Today it houses historical documents, portraits, military artifacts, and exhibits on the Continental Army, Navy, and Marine Corps.

Declaration House (Graff House). The reconstructed Jacob Graff home, where Thomas Jefferson used a room while he drafted the Declaration of Independence.

Liberty Bell Pavilion. Thousands of people each year come here to see this famed symbol of American liberty. The bell tolled on July 8, 1776, to proclaim the first reading of the Declaration of Independence.

Thaddeus Kosciuszko House. The 1797–98 residence of the Polish military engineer who designed important military fortifications at Saratoga and West Point and fought for the American cause during the Revolutionary War.

City Tavern. A reconstruction of America's finest tavern, frequented by the delegates of the First and Second Continental Congresses and the Constitutional Convention of 1787. Within these walls, John Adams, Thomas Jefferson, Benjamin Franklin, George Washington, and others met to discuss the issues of the day.

Washington Square. A monument to the Unknown Soldier of the Revolutionary War stands in this large public park at Sixth and Walnut

Streets. A life-size bronze statue of Gen. George Washington in uniform stands before a stone sarcophagus that holds what are thought to be the remains of a soldier, symbolizing the more than 2,000 soldiers and civilians who died from disease or injury during the war. Flags of the United States and the first thirteen states flank the monument.

Franklin Court. Originally built between 1763 and 1787, the restored complex includes the five Market Street houses once owned by Benjamin Franklin. The complex encompasses an eighteenth-century printing exhibit, a U.S. post office, the *Aurora* newspaper office, and an architectural exhibit. Within the court stands a ghost structure, the outline of Franklin's house with windows looking down on its original foundation. The house was occupied by British officers during Philadelphia's occupation. Beneath the ground is an extensive museum that depicts Franklin's accomplishments through a film, innovative exhibits, historic artifacts, and displays.

Christ Church. This Episcopal Church, built in 1727, is an outstanding example of early Georgian architecture. The church was attended by fifteen signers of the Declaration of Independence, among them George Washington and Benjamin Franklin. Its burial grounds contain the graves of Franklin and four other signers of the Declaration.

When to visit: Most buildings at Independence National Historical Park are open daily, 9 A.M. to 5 P.M. Admission to Independence Hall is by ticket only, available free at the visitors center.

Admission fees: For Second Bank Portrait Gallery, Todd House, and Bishop White House, adults $2. Other sites free.

Special events: Numerous events take place in this busy park. Check the events calendar at the visitors center or on the park's website. March: reenactment of John Adams's inauguration as president at Congress Hall; July 4: Independence Day celebration including ceremony at the Liberty Bell, awarding of Philadelphia's Liberty Medal, band music, military drills, and fireworks; July 8: public reading of the Declaration of Independence at Independence Hall; summer months: outdoor dramas using historic buildings as backdrops.

Tours of the site: Interpretive rangers on duty at most historic buildings.

Time needed to visit: A full day.

Special considerations: A number of buildings are handicapped accessible.

Parking: Parking for a fee in municipal garage on Second Street near visitors center.

Gift shop: Books, maps, art, memorabilia, and children's material.

Each year on July 8, the Declaration of Independence is proclaimed anew outside Independence Hall by a costumed park interpreter.

Directions: From I-95 northbound, take the exit marked Historic Area. Follow the signs for Sixth Street to Chestnut Street, and turn left. Follow Chestnut Street to Second Street, and turn right to parking garage. From I-95 southbound take exit 17 to I-676 following signs to Independence Hall, right on Callowhill Street, left on Sixth Street, left on Chestnut Street to Second Street, right to parking garage. From I-76 eastbound take I-676 to Eighth Street exit south to Race Street, left to Second Street, right to parking garage.

Tourist information
Philadelphia Convention and Visitors Center, Sixteenth and John F. Kennedy Boulevard, telephone 800-537-7676 or 215-636-1666, website www.libertynet.org/phila-visitor.

Other nearby sites
Elfreth's Alley. Located between Second and Front Streets north of Arch Street, this street is lined with restored homes dating from days of William Penn, many still lived in today. A museum at 126 Elfreth's Alley tells the story of the buildings and historic street. Open Tuesday through Sunday for admission fee. For more information, call 215-574-0560.

Betsy Ross House. Restored home of the seamstress who reputedly stitched the first American flag, located at 239 Arch Street. Open Tuesday through Sunday. For more information, call 215-627-5343.

Atwater Kent Museum. Dedicated to the history and archaeology of Philadelphia. Open on Monday, Wednesday, and Sunday from 10 A.M. to 4 P.M. Admission fee. Located at 15 South Seventh Street. For more information, call 215-922-3031.

Fairmount Park. Covers 8,579 acres on both sides of the Schuylkill River and is threaded by scenic drives and walking and bridle trails. Founded in 1812, the park hosted the Centennial Exposition in Memorial Hall, which still stands today. The Mann Center for Performing Arts hosts outdoor concerts by the Philadelphia Orchestra and others. The boathouses along the river are lighted at night and are one of Philadelphia's best-known sites. Historic and restored homes are open for tours. For more information, call 215-684-7922.

National Archives Philadelphia Branch. Contains American history documents from the First Continental Congress to the present time, including Revolutionary War and Civil War records, as well as changing exhibitions. Located at 900 Market Street. Open daily.

Civil War Library and Museum. Research library and museum of Civil War artifacts. One room is dedicated to Abraham Lincoln. Other major exhibits honor Gen. George G. Meade and Gen. Ulysses S. Grant. Military uniforms, histories, flags, pictures, and insignia are displayed. Open Wednesday through Sunday, 11 A.M. to 4:30 P.M. Located at 1805 Pine Street. For more information, call 215-735-8196. (See Civil War—pages 133–70.)

Laurel Hill Cemetery. A national historic landmark founded in 1836, contains 95 acres of gravestones, obelisks, and monuments in a public garden setting. A walking tour points out the graves of thirty-one Civil War generals, including George G. Meade. Open Tuesday through Saturday, 9:30 A.M. to 1:30 P.M. Located on Ridge Avenue between Allegheny and Huntingdon Avenues. For more information, call 215-228-8200.

Fort Roberdeau

R.D. 3, Box 391
Altoona, PA 16601
814-946-0048

The American Revolution had been grinding on for three years.
George Washington's troops had just struggled through a winter of
privation and toughening up at Valley Forge. The American losses at
Brandywine and Germantown had allowed the British to spend the
winter comfortably in Philadelphia and forced Congress to move to
York.

At this juncture, the situation looked grim for the rebelling colonists. The Continental Army was short of everything, not only shoes
for the men at Valley Forge, but even ammunition for their muskets.

One member of the Continental Congress thought he knew a way
to help. Before the outbreak of hostilities with the mother country,
Daniel Roberdeau had been a successful merchant in Philadelphia. He
imported and sold rum, sugar, molasses, wine, and flour from the West
Indies, where he had been born. During the war, he also owned a half
interest in a privateer, an armed vessel that captured an enemy ship
carrying $22,000 in silver, a windfall profit that he patriotically turned
over to Congress to help defray the costs of the war.

A civic leader, he sided early with the Revolutionaries. Soon
after the colonists declared war on England, Roberdeau was elected a
member of Philadelphia's Committee of Safety, along with Benjamin
Franklin, Robert Morris, and others. In 1776, he was elected a brigadier
general and served in the field with Washington during the campaign
in New Jersey. He was elected to the Continental Congress in 1777
and reelected in 1778.

In the spring of 1778, Roberdeau made a proposal to Congress. He
knew the Continental Army was in great need of lead to make bullets
for its muskets. Lead mines in the colonies were scarce, and production
had fallen off. Roberdeau knew of a potentially productive lead source
in western Pennsylvania, on the frontier at the foot of the Allegheny
Mountains near what is now Altoona.

Getting the go-ahead from Congress, along with a vague promise
that it would repay him for his expenses, Roberdeau took a leave of
absence from Congress at York, gathered together a group of men and
materials, and made his way to the lead site on the Juniata River.

Roberdeau realized that to retain the men he had brought out to the frontier, as well as provide the local inhabitants greater safety from Indian and Tory attacks, he needed to build a fort for protection. "I intend to build such a fort as, under the smile of Providence, would enable me to defend it against any number of Indians that might presume to invest it," he wrote, adding that he would erect "a stockade fort if I could stir up the inhabitants to give their labor in furnishing asylum for their families in case of imminent danger and thus prevent evacuation of the country."

He succeeded in getting the workforce to build the stockade and a smelter to melt the lead ore. Ore was dug from pits nearby and brought to the fort, where it was smelted into ingots. These were packed on horses and taken to the Juniata, where they were rafted downriver. Mining operations continued for about two years, producing more than 2,000 pounds of lead. But the lead deposits were poorer than anticipated, payment from the government was delayed, and it became increasingly expensive to mine and smelt the lead ore. In addition, some workmen were bribed by British loyalists into deserting.

These factors led to the abandonment of the mining operation in the autumn of 1779. In the meantime, Roberdeau himself had returned to his seat in Congress. The fort he had constructed, however, continued to serve as a refuge during Indian raids as well as an important base for local troops operating against the Indians.

As was the case with many frontier forts, Fort Roberdeau consisted of a

A Continental soldier and a member of the 8th Pennsylvania Regiment discuss the lead smelter at Fort Roberdeau. The smelter in the rear separated lead for bullets from the ore by the heat from log fires.

Grenadiers of the 42nd Royal Highlander Regiment fire a volley at a Roberdeau reenactment. The grenadiers wear bearskin hats to make them appear more formidable to the enemy. Many Scotsmen were recruited into the British Army after 1745, when the clan system in Scotland was abolished and the English decreed that Scotsmen could wear their kilts only while serving overseas with the army.

number of log buildings surrounded by a log stockade wall. An early sketch shows one difference, however. The fort's walls were constructed of horizontal timbers laid up to a height of 12 to 14 feet. The logs were set horizontally instead of vertically because the fort was built on rocky ground and logs could not be driven in vertically.

Five distinct sections of timbers make up the four stockade walls, the east wall accommodating a gate. On each corner is a small bastion with a platform built into it to give riflemen a good firing location. Within the fort are several structures as well as the smelter. The walls are pierced with loopholes, through which small arms could be fired. A sturdily built brick-and-stone magazine within the enclosure holds the fort's ammunition.

The fort in these years was under the command of Maj. Robert Cluggage, an experienced officer. He had been in active military service since the beginning of the Revolution, having been commissioned in June 1775. He commanded a company during the siege of Boston, then later resigned and returned home to the Maryland-Pennsylvania border.

In 1778, he was commissioned a major and charged with defending this frontier area.

The troops he commanded were members of the local militia and ranger companies, as well as volunteers. The garrison at Fort Roberdeau could be maintained only by rotating short-term militia units. Like many a frontier fort, Roberdeau was not garrisoned with a sufficient number of men to defend the post against a major attack at all times. But in spite of this thin line of defenders, the frontier fort served its purpose of protecting the miners while they unearthed the lead needed to make bullets for the Continental Army. On the frontier, the success of the Patriots rested on effective collection of information by their scouts, or rangers, who watched the Indian trails and raised the alarm in case the settlers needed to take refuge when Iroquois raiding parties moved through the valley.

WHAT YOU SEE TODAY

Today's restored Fort Roberdeau is the result of an ambitious project undertaken by Blair County to commemorate the Bicentennial of the American Revolution in 1976. Fort Roberdeau Historic Site and Natural Area, a Blair County park, now includes the reconstructed log stockade and cabins of the 1778 lead mines fort; a nearby 1858 bank barn with a visitor orientation area, a bookshop, and museum exhibits; a nineteenth-century farmhouse; and an administrative and conference center. The site is listed on the National Register of Historic Places. In addition, five nature trails wind through 47 acres of forest and fields, with outdoor classrooms and picnic areas.

Visitors can tour the reconstructed stockade and go into the officers' quarters, barracks, blacksmith shed, corner bastions, storehouse, lead miners' hut, smelter, and powder magazine. An eight-minute video provides an orientation to the site. Talks and demonstrations are occasionally given in the fort and on the main floor of the barn.

When to visit: May through October, Tuesday to Saturday, 11 A.M. to 5 P.M.; Sunday and Monday, 1 P.M. to 5 P.M.
Admission fees: Adults $3, seniors $2.50, children $1.
Special events: July 4: Independence Day picnic; July: Revolutionary War battle reenactments on Saturdays and Sundays, military demonstrations, camp life, sutlers' tents, children's games, music, and dancing; second Sundays, June through September: special programs on the people and environment of historic Fort Roberdeau.

Tours of the site: Given by staff members.
Time needed to visit: Two hours.
Special considerations: Handicapped accessible.
Parking: Free.
Gift shop: Books, pamphlets, and eighteenth-century merchandise.
Directions: The fort is 8.5 miles northeast of Altoona. From I-99, take the Bellwood exit, and follow signs to the park.

Tourist information

Allegheny Mountains Convention and Visitors Bureau, Logan Valley Mall, U.S. Route 220 and Goods Lane, Altoona, PA 16602, telephone 814-943-4183 or 800-84-ALTOONA, website www.amcvb.com.

Other nearby sites

Lincoln Caverns. Visitors can tour the passageways and chambers of a limestone cavern discovered by highway workers in 1930 in nearby Huntingdon. Whisper Rocks, Meditation Chapel, and the annual Ghosts and Goblins Tours in October are some of the highlights. For more information, call 814-643-0268.

Baker Mansion. The nineteenth-century Greek Revival home of ironmaster Elias Baker, today home of the Blair County Historical Society in Altoona. Open for tours Tuesday, Thursday, and Friday, beginning April 1. For more information, call 814-942-3916.

Altoona Railroaders Memorial Museum. Displays locomotives and railroad cars and illustrates the development of the Pennsylvania Railroad through interactive exhibits and a model railroad. Located at 1300 Ninth Avenue in Altoona. For more information, call 888-4-ALTOONA or visit the website www.railroadcity.com.

Horseshoe Curve National Historic Landmark. This engineering marvel, opened by the Pennsylvania Railroad in 1854, 6 miles west of Altoona, made it possible for transcontinental steam locomotives to surmount the Allegheny Mountains. For more information, call 888-4-ALTOONA or visit the website www.railroadcity.com.

Allegheny Portage Railway National Historic Site. Inclined railway that began operating in 1834 in Cresson. Travel between Philadelphia and Pittsburgh over the Allegheny Mountains was reduced from three weeks by wagon to four days by railroad and canal. Flatbed railcars transported canal boats over a mountain ridge to continue their trip by canal across the state. For more information, call 814-886-6150.

Washington Crossing
Historic Park

Box 103
Washington Crossing, PA 18977
215-493-4076
fax: 215-493-4820
website: www.spiritof76.com

These were perhaps the darkest days of the American Revolution. A year and a half had elapsed since the rebellion began, when the armed minutemen had fired on the British redcoats at Lexington and Concord, Massachusetts. Only recently, Gen. George Washington and his poorly supplied, poorly clothed army had suffered defeat at the Battle of Long Island in New York. Now they had retreated during cold, wet December weather across New Jersey to reach the relative safety of the Pennsylvania side of the Delaware River.

To make matters worse, the enlistments of many of the Continental soldiers were due to conclude at the end of the year, and they would return to their homes. As Thomas Paine, the well-known pamphleteer, wrote at the time, "These are the times that try men's souls." To many Americans, things seemed to be so bad that they thought the war for independence might soon be over.

Washington, as commander in chief, had to do something to buoy the Americans' flagging morale, and he had to do it before the termination of the enlistments of his men drained away his manpower, so he made an audacious move. On Christmas night in 1776, while most others were relaxing in comfort, he and 2,400 soldiers launched a surprise attack on a garrison of 1,400 Hessian mercenaries who were holding the town of Trenton for the British.

To reach the Jersey shore, the men marched down to the riverbank after dark on Christmas night and piled into sturdy Durham boats, normally used to transport pig iron from forge to market. Experienced fishermen from Massachusetts poled the boats across the river, dodging occasional ice floes and fighting their way through a slanting snowstorm. They also managed to ferry across eighteen cannons and a few horses before the troops began their 9-mile march to Trenton. Two smaller contingents who were to join in the attack turned back in the

Tradition holds that Washington and his officers ate dinner at McConkey's Ferry Inn before they mustered their troops to cross the Delaware River and attack Trenton in 1776. Visitors may tour the restored inn.

face of the snowstorm, leaving Washington to make the attack with his force alone.

As Washington had calculated, the Hessians had been feasting and celebrating Christmas, never suspecting that the forlorn American troops would, or could, attack them. Even though the Hessian commander had been warned of a possible American attack, he slacked off on posting patrols.

In the early morning hours of December 26, the Americans surrounded the village, set up their artillery where it could fire down the two main streets, and effectively cut off most of the Hessians' escape routes. Washington gave the order to advance. The surprised Hessian soldiers tried frantically to form up in ranks to fight. American muskets and rifles blasted from windows along the streets—the Americans had had the forethought in this stormy weather to dry their powder and flints in the warmth of some of the Trenton homes. One rifleman took deadly aim at the Hessian commander, who had been routed from bed only minutes before by the attack, and the German toppled from his horse, mortally wounded. His deputy commander also fell. Leaderless, many of the Hessians soon surrendered.

For the Americans, "only two officers and one or two privates were wounded," Washington reported. Forty Hessians were killed and 400 others escaped to join other British units in New Jersey, but Washington's troops captured 1,000 prisoners, six cannons, 140 horses, 1,000 muskets and rifles, musical instruments, and forty barrels of rum.

It was the first clear-cut triumph by the Continental Army over the veteran British and Hessian forces. "It is a glorious victory," wrote Washington's aide. "It will rejoice the hearts of our friends everywhere and give new life to our hitherto waning fortunes. Washington has baffled the enemy in his retreat from New York. He has pounced upon the Hessians like an eagle upon a hen and is safe once more on this side of the river. If he does nothing more, he will live in history as a great military commander."

Back in England, officials were dismayed at the turn of events. "All our hopes were blasted by that unhappy affair at Trenton," concluded Lord George Germain, the colonial secretary to King George III.

After his troops returned to Pennsylvania after the victory, Washington again appealed to those whose enlistments were ending, asking them to extend long enough to go into battle one more time against the British. Such was the esteem in which he was held by his men that most of them agreed to stay and fight. One week later, evading British reinforcements who had reclaimed Trenton, Washington led his plucky army back to New Jersey, marching 10 miles to Princeton. The Battle of Princeton lasted less than an hour, but it was among the most savage of the war. Again the Americans triumphed, routing a bayonet-wielding British force. Only after these two battles did Washington and his rejuvenated Continental Army march into Morristown and go into their winter encampment.

WHAT YOU SEE TODAY

Visitors Center and Museum. Housed in the Memorial Building, the museum provides information and exhibits about the park. A copy of Emanuel Leutze's famous painting *Washington Crossing the Delaware* hangs on the wall of the auditorium. A twenty-minute film sets the scene of the 1776 event. Exhibits explain eighteenth-century textile making, which was practiced in the village that later grew up here.

Two replica Durham boats are on display near the embarkation point for Washington's river crossing.

McConkey's Old Ferry Inn. Samuel McConkey bought the ferry and the inn in 1774 and was the innkeeper when Washington camped here. It is believed that Washington ate his evening meal on December 25, 1776, at this inn before embarking on the assault. Visitors may tour the restored inn.

Thompson-Neely House. This home was requisitioned for quarters during the encampment for Revolutionary officers Gen. Lord Stirling, Capt. William Washington, Capt. James Moore, and Lt. James Monroe. Captain Washington, the nephew of General Washington, and Monroe were both wounded in the Trenton attack. The furnishings are authentic period pieces, and the house serves as a museum. A nearby road leads over the Delaware Canal to the Memorial Flagstaff, where unknown soldiers of the Continental Army lie buried.

Taylor House. The restored 1816 home of Mahlon Taylor, the son of the founder of Taylorsville, the village that grew up at the site of Washington's crossing. Guided tours are given of the first and second floors.

Bowman's Hill Tower. A lookout was posted here during Washington's encampment of 2,400 soldiers, and a commanding 14-mile view can be seen from the 110-foot tower. Bowman's Hill Wildflower Preserve, a 100-acre sanctuary, has indoor and outdoor exhibits and twenty-six hiking trails.

When to visit: The park is open daily from dawn to dusk. Historic buildings are open Tuesday through Saturday, 9 A.M. to 5 P.M. and Sunday, 12 noon to 5 P.M., except holidays.

Admission fees: Park admission is $1 per private vehicle. Tickets to tour five buildings cost $4 for adults, $2 for children age 6 to 12, and $3 for seniors over age sixty.

Special events: Christmas Day: annual reenactment of the crossing, with troops in period uniforms embarking in replica Durham boats; May: sheepshearing and Colonial Day encampment; October: Heritage Day.

Tours of the site: Tours available of five buildings: the Thompson-Neely House, McConkey Ferry Inn, Hibbs House, Bowman's Hill Tower, and Taylor House.

Time needed to visit: Allow two hours minimum to tour the buildings, plus time to visit the river crossing site.

Parking: At the visitors center.

Gift shop: The Old Ferry Inn offers books, pamphlets, and historical souvenirs. Food is also available. Memorabilia sold at Thompson-Neely House.

Directions: The park is divided into two sections. To reach the Washington Crossing section, take exit 31 of I-95, then travel 3 miles north on Taylorsville Road to PA Route 532; turn right and continue 1 mile to park, which is on PA Route 32. To reach the Thompson-Neely section, drive north from the Washington Crossing section 3 miles on PA Route 32. The Thompson-Neely section is located 1.5 miles southeast of New Hope.

Tourist information

Lehigh Valley Convention and Visitor Bureau, P.O. Box 20785, Lehigh Valley, PA 18002, telephone 800-747-0561 or 610-882-9200, website www.lehighvalleypa.org.

Bucks County Conference and Visitors Bureau, 152 Swamp Road, Doylestown, PA 18901, telephone 800-836-BUCKS or 215-345-4552, website www:bctc.org.

Other nearby sites

Washington Crossing State Park, New Jersey. In the visitors center, a film shows a reenactment of the battles of Trenton and Princeton. Revolutionary War weapons, uniform accessories, military equipment, documents, maps, and currency are displayed in one gallery. Another gallery familiarizes the visitor with events leading up to the outbreak of the Revolutionary War. The nearby Johnson Ferry House is an early eighteenth-century farmhouse and tavern whose owner operated a ferry that crossed the river. The keeping room, bedchamber, and textile room are furnished with local period pieces similar to those the Johnson family would have owned from 1740 to 1770. It is likely that Gen. George Washington held a meeting in the house while his troops disembarked after crossing the river for the attack on Trenton. Located at NJ Route 546 and NJ Route 29 in Titusville. For more information, call 609-737-9303. Open Wednesday to Sunday, 9 A.M. to 4 P.M.

Old Barracks Museum. Interpreters in period dress greet visitors to the recently restored barracks, one of the few surviving military sites from the Battle of Trenton. The tour features audio-visual effects and guides you to a typical barracks room, a hospital room, and officers' quarters. Exhibits explain how archaeologists, architects, and curators restored the historic site. Open daily from 10 A.M. to 5 P.M., except for major holidays. Adults $6, seniors and students $3. Located on

Barracks Street in Trenton, New Jersey. For more information, call 609-396-1776.

Trenton Battle Monument. A 50-foot granite column marks the spot where an artillery battery under Col. Henry Knox shelled the Hessians as they attempted to form up to oppose the attacking Americans. Located at the corner of North Warren Street and North Broad Street.

The David Library of the American Revolution. Has 40,000 books and pamphlets and 10,000 reels of microfilm material dealing with the French and Indian War and the American Revolution. Available for use by scholars and the general public. Conferences and lectures also held. Open Tuesday through Saturday, 10 A.M. to 5 P.M. Located at 1201 River Road in Washington Crossing. For more information, call 215-493-6776.

Pennsbury Manor. The seventeenth-century country estate of William Penn located in Morrisville, overlooking the Delaware River. Costumed guides lead visitors through replicas of the manor house and worker's cottage, smokehouse, blacksmith shop, and other outbuildings. Open Tuesday through Saturday, 9 A.M. to 5 P.M.; Sunday noon to 5 P.M. For more information, call 215-946-0400. Admission fee.

Brandywine Battlefield

P.O. Box 202
Chadds Ford, PA 19317
610-459-3342
fax: 610-459-9586
website: www.ushistory.org/brandywine

For the British Army, ordered to subdue the American colonists who had dared to revolt against the king, the strategy was clear. The British commanding general, Sir William Howe, would land his force of 16,000 men, horses, and artillery at the head of the Chesapeake Bay. Once ashore, they would fight their way the scant 50 miles northward to capture the Colonial capital of Philadelphia. He believed the capture of Philadelphia would greatly weaken the colonists' resolve.

Once this was achieved, Howe's troops would march northward to link up with Gen. John Burgoyne's troops, who were pushing their way down the Hudson Valley from Quebec. When the forces of Howe and Burgoyne met, they would effectively cut off the rebellious New England colonies from the others. The rebel forces would be divided and their capital city occupied, and the Americans would be forced to sue for peace.

So it was with supreme confidence that Howe, his British regulars, and his Hessian, or German, soldiers of fortune marched toward Philadelphia in the fall of 1777. Logically deducing the thrust of Howe's plan, Gen. George Washington took up defensive positions with 11,000 men, many of them hastily mustered militiamen. Washington knew the British would have to cross the eastward-flowing Brandywine Creek to reach Philadelphia, and the main road to Philadelphia crossed the river at John Chad's Ford. He therefore deployed his troops on high ground at the ford, stationing them on the river's north slope, to take advantage of both the height of the terrain and the natural obstacle presented by the river itself. He stationed other forces upstream to the west at the four other fords his scouts had identified.

It was September 10 when the redcoats reached the river. Howe ordered Gen. Wilhelm Knyphausen and several regiments to engage the rebel forces at Chad's Ford, as Washington had anticipated. But while the Americans were meeting this expected challenge, Howe divided his army and led 8,000 of his men on a forced march westward along the south side of the river, toward two lesser-known fords across tribu-

69

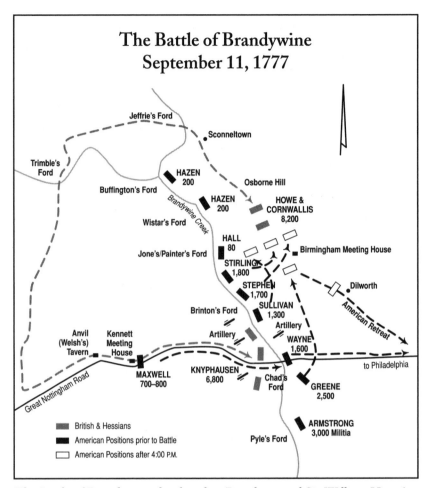

The Battle of Brandywine
September 11, 1777

Jeffrie's Ford

Sconneltown

Trimble's Ford

Buffington's Ford

HAZEN 200

Osborne Hill

HAZEN 200

HOWE & CORNWALLIS 8,200

Wistar's Ford

Brandywine Creek

HALL 80

Birmingham Meeting House

Jone's/Painter's Ford

STIRLING 1,800

STEPHEN 1,700

Dilworth

Brinton's Ford

SULLIVAN 1,300

American Retreat

Artillery

Anvil (Welsh's) Tavern

Kennett Meeting House

Artillery

WAYNE 1,600

MAXWELL 700–800

KNYPHAUSEN 6,800

Chad's Ford

to Philadelphia

Great Nottingham Road

GREENE 2,500

◼ British & Hessians

◼ American Positions prior to Battle

▢ American Positions after 4:00 P.M.

Pyle's Ford

ARMSTRONG 3,000 Militia

The Battle of Brandywine developed as British general Sir William Howe's forces outflanked the Continentals, crossed Brandywine Creek, and forced the Americans to fall back. Both sides suffered heavy losses.

taries of the river. Loyalist sympathizers had revealed these fords to the British. This flanking end run caught the American defenders by surprise. Washington's scouts got no warning of these British movements from the Quaker farmers of the area, who undoubtedly saw the redcoat columns. The Quakers, who strongly opposed war of any kind, maintained a stolid neutrality throughout the rebellion.

Once he realized that Howe had split his forces and had caught him in a two-pronged pincers movement, Washington ordered several contingents to engage the British, who had now crossed the river to the north side and had reached the Quaker meetinghouse at Birmingham. Fighting raged at both ends of the pincers, combat described by one British officer as "a most infernal fire of cannon and musquetry . . . incessant shouting . . . the balls ploughing up the ground, the trees cracking over one's head, the branches riven by artillery, the leaves falling as in autumn by their grapeshot."

Even though Washington rushed in with reinforcements to bolster his battle lines, the Colonials were forced to fall back before the superior British attack. Casualties were heavy on both sides; both American and British wounded men were later treated at a field hospital set up at the Birmingham Friends Meeting House. The newly arrived French officer, Marquis de Lafayette, attempted to rally the Americans but was himself wounded in the left calf and was carried off to have his injury treated. The twenty-year-old French aristocrat had volunteered to join the Continental Army out of a desire for glory and dissatisfaction at events in France. Later, as he gained experience, he became a trusted aide to Washington.

Refighting the Battle of Brandywine, troops oppose each other at the annual reenactment at Brandywine Battlefield State Park. Troops on the left side of the British unit in the foreground reload their muskets after firing, while those on the right prepare to fire a volley. "Wounded" soldiers lie on the ground.

Toward evening, a cavalry charge by the Americans, combined with continuing heavy shelling by the Colonial artillery, stopped Howe's advance. The British savored their victory and did not pursue the retreating Colonial Army after dark over unfamiliar terrain.

The Americans, although surprised and outnumbered, had not been routed. Brandywine, however, turned out to be the biggest land battle of the six-year war, and one of the few engagements where Washington directly faced Britain's top commander, Maj. Gen. William Howe. American casualties were estimated at 1,300; British casualties were almost 2,000.

After spending several days treating their wounded and burying their dead, the victorious redcoats marched on toward Philadelphia, leaving behind butchered local farm animals, pillaged stores of grain, and ransacked homes. On September 26, the main British force marched into Philadelphia unopposed.

WHAT YOU SEE TODAY

Visitors Center. Washington's first line of defense is preserved at Brandywine Battlefield State Park at Chadds Ford (another "d" was later added to the town's name). The best place to start your tour is at the park visitors center. Interpretive exhibits and a film tell the story of the battle and its relationship to the fall of Philadelphia, introduce the military personalities involved, and describe the armaments used in the conflict. A Ferguson rifle, an advanced weapon at the time, is on display. This weapon, a breech-loading rifle rather than the slow-to-load smoothbore musket of the day, was invented by a British officer, Maj. Patrick Ferguson. Only a few of them, however, ever reached the British soldiers. Ferguson was later killed at the Battle of King's Mountain, and the British never capitalized on this superior weapon.

Gideon Gilpin House. The farmhouse where Lafayette, the French aristocrat who volunteered with the American army, was billeted has been restored and contains period furnishings. The farm was plundered after the battle by foraging British soldiers. It was owned by a Quaker farmer, a pacifist, who sought to remain neutral during the battle but lost "10 milk cows, one yoke of oxen, 48 sheep, 28 swine, 12 tons of hay, 230 bushels of wheat, 50 pounds of bacon, a history book and one gun." A huge sycamore tree that grew there at the time still stands nearby.

Benjamin Ring House. This reconstructed farmhouse of a prosperous Quaker farmer and miller was used by General Washington as his headquarters during the battle. On September 9, 1777, Washington held a council of war here to coordinate strategy for the coming

engagement. The house was later reconstructed to its original specifica-
tions after it was destroyed by fire.

Birmingham Friends Meeting House. This old stone meetinghouse, near the park, stood in the midst of the heaviest fighting during
the battle. Constructed in 1763, it was commandeered by the Americans as a field hospital before the battle; as the fighting raged around
it, both American and British wounded were treated here by doctors.
Some of its doors were even removed from their hinges to serve as
stretchers. Visitors are welcome today to visit the meetinghouse, which
still serves an active congregation. Adjacent is a walled cemetery. A
low granite block marks the common grave of a number of unknown
dead of both sides. In another section of the cemetery stands an imposing monument to Lafayette.

When to visit: Open year-round Tuesday through Saturday, 9 A.M. to
5 P.M., Sunday, 12 noon to 5 P.M. Closed Monday except Memorial
Day and Labor Day. Park grounds open later during summer.

Admission fees: Admission to visitors center free. Tours: Adults
$3.50, seniors $2.50, children $1.50. Van tour: $15.

Special events: Second weekend of September: reenactment of a
Revolutionary War battle; spring and fall: narrated van tours of the
battlefield; first Saturday in December: candlelight guided tours of
the historic buildings and tours of local eighteenth-century homes
in the area; February: history talks each Thursday evening; June,
July, and August: summer history camp for children.

Tours of the site: Offered daily.

Time needed to visit: Two hours.

Special considerations: Visitors center is handicapped accessible. All
buildings smoke free.

Parking: Free.

Gift shop: Books, pamphlets, videos, cassettes, and memorabilia.

Directions: Entrance on U.S. Route 1, 2 miles west of PA Route 202
in Chadds Ford.

Tourist information

Chester County Tourist Bureau, Government Services Center,
601 Westtown Road, Suite 170, West Chester, PA 19382, telephone
610-344-5365 or 800-228-9933.

Brandywine Valley Tourist Information Center, in the Longwood
Meeting House off U.S. Route 1 by Longwood Gardens, telephone 610-
388-2900 or 800-228-9933, website www.brandywinevalley.com.

Delaware County Convention and Visitor Bureau, 200 East State Street, Media, PA 19063, telephone 610-565-3679 or 800-343-3983, website www.delcocvb.org.

Other nearby sites

Barnes-Brinton House. A restored eighteenth-century tavern that offers Colonial craft demonstrations during the summer. Located on U.S. Route 1 in Chadds Ford. For more information, call 610-388-7376.

Brandywine River Museum. A nineteenth-century gristmill converted into a museum of American art, featuring the paintings of three generations of the Wyeth family. On U.S. Route 1 south of PA Route 100 in Chadds Ford. Open daily except Christmas. For more information call 610-388-2700 for information on special exhibits.

Longwood Gardens. Once the country estate of Francis Du Pont, now open to the public, with over 1,000 acres of horticultural displays, fountains, two lakes, woodlands, formal gardens, greenhouses and conservatories. Located at U.S. Route 1 and PA Route 52, 3 miles northeast of Kennett Square. For more information, call 610-388-1000 or 800-737-5500.

John Chad House. The restored 1725 stone house of John Chad, now headquarters for the Chadds Ford Historical Society. Located on PA Route 100 west of Chadds Ford. Summer weekend programs are offered. For more information, call 610-388-7376.

Colonial Pennsylvania Plantation. A working plantation for over three hundred years. Restored to its eighteenth-century appearance, with animals and farming typical of the period, it is described by costumed historical interpreters. On weekends from April to November, visitors can observe farm family cooking, food preservation, and the tending of field crops. Located in Ridley Creek State Park on PA Route 3 in Media. For more information, call 610-566-1725.

Paoli Memorial Grounds

Malvern Borough Hall
First and Warren Avenues
Malvern, PA 19355
610-644-2602

After the Battle of Brandywine, the British army moved to nearby Dilworthtown, sending its wounded to Wilmington in Delaware. After a few days, the redcoats continued their advance toward their main objective, the Continental capital of Philadelphia.

Washington and his forces maneuvered toward the Schuylkill River as he endeavored to keep his army between the British and Philadelphia. To slow the British advance, he detached a division of 1,500 soldiers under the command of Brig. Gen. Anthony Wayne to harass the British on their march. Knowing that Wayne's men would be close to the redcoats, Washington warned them to be wary of ambushes.

In accordance with his orders, Wayne marched his men at dawn on September 19 toward the British camp at Tredyffrin. He hoped to find the British preparing to break camp; this would be a time when they would be most vulnerable to a quick attack. "But when we arrived within a half-mile of their encampment found they had not stirred but lay too compact to admit of an attack with prudence."

Deciding against an attack at that time, Wayne withdrew his force and set up a secluded camp of his own in a setting of farm fields surrounded by dense woods near the Warren and Paoli taverns and about 4 miles away from the British. Here he expected to soon be reinforced by a contingent of militiamen from Maryland. With these added numbers, he planned to attack the British on September 21. He had received reports that his foe intended to march onward toward Philadelphia.

Wayne felt secure in his position, even though he knew he was close to the enemy. He knew the neighborhood intimately, since his home, Waynesborough, was only a few miles away. While he waited for the Maryland militia to arrive and for the main British force to break camp and leave, he took the usual precautions of posting pickets to warn him of any enemy movements. He was warned by a local farmer on the evening of September 20 that the British planned an attack that night on the American camp. Although skeptical of the report, Wayne sent out additional pickets to cover all sides of his camp and posted horsemen to patrol the roads.

Meanwhile, the British commander, Maj. Gen. Charles Grey, with a force of 1,200 soldiers, had been ordered to attack the Americans. He came up with an unusual plan for the assault. From his spies, he had a good idea of the location of Wayne's encampment and forced a local blacksmith to lead him there. He then divided his force in order to attack the camp from two sides. He launched the assault late at night to try to catch the Americans sleeping and forbade his soldiers from firing their muskets—they could use only their bayonets. A British staff officer explained why: "By not firing we knew the foe to be wherever fire appeared and a charge ensured his destruction; that amongst the Enemy those in the rear would direct their fire against whoever fired in front, and they would destroy each other."

It was just past midnight on a rainy night when Grey's force pressed its attack in the darkness. They overwhelmed the outlying pickets, killing or capturing them, but not before the pickets had fired several shots, thus alerting Wayne's men back at the camp. The Americans scrambled to form up to meet the impending attack.

When the assault came, the Colonials fought back but could not fully form their ranks to fire before the bayonet-wielding redcoats closed in. A British officer recalled the scene: "The whole battalion dashed into the wood, and guided by the straggling fire of the picket, that was followed close up, we entered the camp and gave such a cheer as made the wood echo. The enemy were completely surprised; some with arms, others without, running in all directions in the greatest confusion. The light infantry bayoneted every man they came up with. The camp was immediately set on fire, and this, with the cries of the wounded, formed together one of the most dreadful scenes I ever beheld."

The American defenses dissolved as Wayne's troops fled westward for safety. Many more fell dead or wounded or were taken prisoner. Some of the American soldiers, silhouetted by their own campfires, became easy targets for British bayonets. The scene was a grisly one punctuated by screams and the clashing of swords and bayonets rather than the crack of musket shots. The attackers set fire to American huts, forcing some who had hidden within to flee or be killed.

In the turmoil, Wayne managed to save his artillery pieces and formed up his light infantry to cover the retreat. Some Continental soldiers scattered across the countryside, but most of the defending force managed to stay intact. The Americans lost 53 killed and about 100 wounded. The British carried off 71 prisoners, 40 of whom were wounded. The victorious British suffered only 4 killed and 8 to 20 wounded.

The rout of the American contingent removed the last obstacle to General Howe's capture of Philadelphia. He marched his army across the Schuylkill River at Fatland Ford (the water at the time was only a foot deep) and on September 25 marched triumphantly into a capital that had been evacuated by the Continental Congress and by other patriots and their supporters. Washington and the rest of the Continental Army had already crossed to the north shore of the river, where they were in no position to challenge the British advance.

WHAT YOU SEE TODAY

Two monuments at Paoli Memorial Grounds, on Monument Road in Malvern, overlook the original encampment of Wayne's soldiers. The site remains cultivated farmland, as it was then. An original monument commemorates the death of fifty-three American soldiers killed in the Paoli Battle on September 20, 1777. It stands atop a large mound that covers a mass grave, hastily dug at the time to bury the dead. The barrels of two Revolutionary War cannons stand guard at the entrance to the monument, which is surrounded by a stone wall. A second, larger monument was later erected in 1877 because the text of the original was becoming illegible. The later monument bears the legend: "Sacred to the memory of the patriots who on this spot fell, a sacrifice to British barbarity during the struggle for American independence on the night of the 20th of September, 1777."

A monument, encased in protective plastic, stands atop a large mound that holds the bodies of the Revolutionary soldiers slain in 1777 during the nighttime battle.

When to visit: Always.
Admission fees: Free.
Tours of the site: Self-guided.
Time needed to visit: Half an hour.
Special considerations: Handicapped accessible.
Parking: Free parking available at the site.
Directions: Take U.S. Route 30 (Lancaster Pike) west to Paoli; turn left on King Street. In the borough of Malvern, turn left on Malvern Street. Go two blocks to Monument Avenue, and turn left. Park entrance is on Monument Avenue.

Other nearby sites

Waynesborough. The birthplace and home of Gen. Anthony Wayne is located 1 mile south of U.S. Route 30 and PA Route 252 at 2049 Waynesborough Road. The restored Georgian home is furnished with period furniture and objects belonging to Wayne. Open Tuesday, Thursday, and Sunday from March to December. For more information, call 610-647-1779.

Historic Yellow Springs. Restored eighteenth- and nineteenth-century village and health spa on Art Spring Road in Chester Springs. The ruins of a Revolutionary War hospital are evident. Yellow Springs continues as an art community. For more information, call 610-827-7414.

Chester County Historical Society. An outstanding historical resource, with five galleries, interactive exhibits, extensive research library, educational programs, and museum shop. Located at 225 North High Street in West Chester. For more information, call 610-692-4800.

Fort Mifflin

Fort Mifflin Road
Philadelphia, PA 19153
215-492-1881
215-685-4192 (public information)
fax: 215-492-1608

By the end of September 1777, the British forces under Gen. William Howe had defeated the Americans at the Battle of Brandywine. They caught them off guard at Paoli, compelled Gen. George Washington's army to retreat to the countryside, and occupied the colonists' capital city of Philadelphia, where they settled down for the winter.

The war seemed to be going Howe's way. The British commander had one major problem, however, which would soon become evident. Supplies could not reach his army from New York by water because the Americans were blocking the Delaware River below Philadelphia with obstructions, forts, and small armed vessels. If the Americans continued to prevent British ships from sailing up the river to Philadelphia, the British army would suffer because wagon trains that brought supplies by land from Maryland or across New Jersey were vulnerable to attack.

As part of their river defenses, the Americans had constructed barriers across the river at two places. They had deployed a series of underwater obstacles called *chevaux-de-frise,* iron-tipped spikes embedded in a framework of rocks that rested on the river bottom. These spikes, protruding just beneath the surface, could rip into the bottom of a ship that tried to sail over them. If any ship managed to make its way through these underwater barriers, it would have to run a gauntlet between two forts: Fort Mifflin, on the Pennsylvania side of the river, and Fort Mercer, on the New Jersey side. The twin forts were located just south of where the Delaware River meets the Schuylkill River.

Fort Mifflin, constructed partly of stone walls, partly log stockade, was built on a low-lying island off the Pennsylvania shore. Most of its cannons were aimed toward the river channel to protect the city against enemy ships. Across the river, facing Fort Mifflin, was Fort Mercer, a well-built redoubt with high earthen walls surrounded by ditches and abatis (pointed stakes designed to discourage an assault by foot soldiers). Between the two forts, an iron chain stretched across the river to keep unwanted ships from moving upstream. In order to bring in the

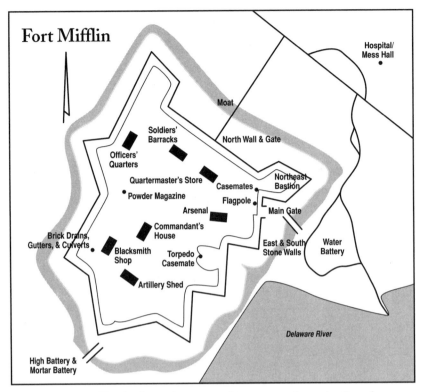

Fort Mifflin

- Hospital/Mess Hall
- Moat
- Soldiers' Barracks
- North Wall & Gate
- Officers' Quarters
- Quartermaster's Store
- Casemates
- Northeast Bastion
- Powder Magazine
- Flagpole
- Arsenal
- Main Gate
- Brick Drains, Gutters, & Culverts
- Commandant's House
- East & South Stone Walls
- Water Battery
- Blacksmith Shop
- Torpedo Casemate
- Artillery Shed
- Delaware River
- High Battery & Mortar Battery

Plan of Fort Mifflin discloses that most of its cannon batteries face the Delaware River, not toward land, where the British attackers placed their artillery.

supplies his troops needed, General Howe had to clear away all of these obstacles and eliminate the small fleet of armed vessels with which the Americans patrolled the river.

By mid-October, the British had succeeded in removing enough of the first barrier of *chevaux-de-frise* to allow their warships to sail upriver far enough that the ships could add their firepower to the British can-nons ashore. After removing this first obstacle, they tackled Fort Mercer—with disastrous results. The British ordered a force of 1,200 of their German mercenaries, known as Hessians, to capture Fort Mercer, which was defended by about 1,000 Americans. After shelling the fort with their cannons, the Germans attempted to scale the fort's walls at three places but were beaten back at each location. The Americans poured murderous fire down on the attackers from their protected posi-tions. More than 370 of the Germans were killed or wounded, and at least 120 were captured or reported missing in what is also known as the Battle of Red Bank. The American losses were only 14 killed and 23 wounded. Fort Mercer remained under American control.

Meanwhile, the British were frustrated on the river as well. To try to bring more firepower to bear and to support the attack upon Fort Mercer, they had sailed several warships upriver past the first line of *chevaux-de-frise*. But the river was narrow, shoals were uncharted, and the wind was blowing the wrong way. As a result, two warships ran aground. The Americans took advantage of their helplessness to attack them with floating gun batteries and with cannon fire from Fort Mifflin. The 64-gun warship *Augusta* was set afire and blown up, while the British themselves set afire another ship to keep it from falling into American hands. With things going against them, the other British ships withdrew downriver.

After these setbacks, the British turned their attention to Fort Mifflin. This time the British made sure they had superiority in firepower and set about pounding the fort into submission. Over the previous few weeks, they had installed several cannon batteries along the Pennsylvania shoreline less than a mile from Fort Mifflin. These cannons began firing at the fort on November 9, 1777.

To this cannonade from the shoreline was added a shower of shot from a 16-gun floating battery on the river, which they had towed into place only a few yards offshore. Six other warships sailed in to lob cannonballs into the fort. Sometimes as many as a thousand cannonballs an hour landed within the beleaguered fort. The thunder of guns shook buildings in Philadelphia and could be heard across the river in New Jersey.

The 300 defenders of Fort Mifflin could offer little but bravery against this onslaught. Like all forts, Mifflin had most of its guns pointed toward the river to protect against approaching warships. Only four cannons faced the Pennsylvania shore, and the two largest of these were knocked out of action in the first minutes of the fight.

By the end of the third day of the bombardment, most of the ramparts facing Pennsylvania were smashed beyond repair. Only one gun, a 32-pounder, was left that could reach the British land batteries. Soon the Americans ran out of ammunition entirely. In desperation, the story goes, soldiers ran into the yard, picked up unexploded British 32-pound cannonballs, and fired them back at their opponents.

The British maneuvered their floating battery closer to the besieged fort. Marksmen in her topmasts felled a number of the fort's defenders

Two militiamen prepare to take part in the annual reenactment of the bombardment of Fort Mifflin.

with musket shots and hand grenades. Nevertheless, the fort's garrison held on until dark on the fifth day, its flag still flying from what one soldier described as "an old ship's mast, having shrouds to the ground, and the round top still remaining."

Finally, after dark on November 15, the fewer than 100 survivors evacuated the ruined fort. Salvaging about ten cannons, they loaded them onto a barge and tried to sneak it past the British warships—to no avail as the barge was discovered and sent to the bottom by cannon fire. The Americans deliberately left the garrison flag still flying over the crumbled fort as they left, a symbol that the fort had never surrendered. The next morning, a British landing party took the Colonial flag down and raised the Union Jack.

With the loss of Fort Mifflin to the British, only Fort Mercer remained in American hands. Within days, the British landed 6,000 fresh troops in New Jersey and advanced on Fort Mercer. Seeing that they would be overpowered, the Americans blew up the fort, denying it to the British. The Americans also set seventeen boats afire that had taken part in the river defense. On November 26, the British cut the chain that stretched across the river and sixty-two ships of the British fleet sailed triumphantly up to Philadelphia's docks.

The stubborn resistance of the defenders of the two forts and those who manned the impromptu fleet of armed river craft had prevented Howe from resupplying his troops in Philadelphia. The lack of supplies and munitions, in turn, prevented the British from mounting further attacks to try to destroy Washington's lurking army.

WHAT YOU SEE TODAY

Fort Mifflin, recognized as a National Historic Landmark, has been carefully restored to its early-nineteenth-century appearance. It incorporates some of the stone walls of the fortification. Visitors can walk atop the battlements and look through the restored buildings, including the officers' quarters, enlisted men's barracks, quartermaster's store, artillery shed, and casemates. A museum includes interpretive exhibits describing the Revolutionary War siege, a diorama of the fort, and an exhibit of the *chevaux-de-frise*. A slide show relates the history of the fort.

When to visit: Open April 1 to November 30, Wednesday through Sunday, 10 A.M. to 4 P.M.

Admission fees: Adults $5, seniors $4.50, children $2.

Special events: Around July 4: Fort Mifflin Freedom Blast. Reenactments, living-history demonstrations, and events commemorating several wars. Uniform and weapons demonstrations.

Tours of the site: Tours by uniformed guides or self-guided.

Time needed to visit: Two hours.

Special considerations: Handicapped accessible.

Parking: Free.

Gift shop: Books, booklets, and memorabilia.

Directions: Located near Philadelphia International Airport, just off I-95. Take the Island Avenue exit, then go .5 mile south to Fort Mifflin Road and follow the signs.

Other nearby sites

Red Bank Battlefield. Park preserving the remnants of Fort Mercer and the 1748 Whitall House. The house is open year-round, Wednesday, 9 A.M. to 4 P.M. and Saturday and Sunday, 1 P.M. to 4 P.M. Located across the Delaware River in National Park, New Jersey. For more information, call 609-853-5120.

Historic Bartram's Gardens. The eighteenth-century farm of Colonial botanist John Bartram, now a 44-acre public park along the Schuylkill River. Featured are the Bartram house, botanical gardens, and a wildflower meadow. Reached from Lindbergh Boulevard west of 54th Street in South Philadelphia. For more information, call 215-729-5281 or visit website www.libertynet.org/~bartram.

John Heinz National Wildlife Refuge at Tinicum. An environmental education center preserving Tinicum Marsh, the largest remaining tidal wetland in Pennsylvania. The area was first settled in 1643 by the Swedes, Dutch, and English, who diked and drained the marsh for grazing. Today visitors watch wildlife and migrating birds from trails, boardwalks, and observation platforms. Located at 86th Street and Lindburgh Boulevard in southwest Philadelphia, adjacent to the Philadelphia International Airport, the refuge is open year-round from 8:30 A.M. to 4 P.M. For more information, call 215-365-3118.

Cliveden

BATTLE OF GERMANTOWN

6401 Germantown Avenue
Philadelphia, PA 19144
215-848-1777
website: www.cliveden.org

Despite the British occupation of the Continental capital city of Philadelphia and the recent defeats on the battlegrounds of Brandywine and Paoli, the indomitable general George Washington set about making plans for yet another assault against the British. In this he was heartened by the arrival of reinforcements, which increased his strength to some 10,000 soldiers, about 7,000 of them Continental soldiers, the remainder local militiamen.

By early October 1777, Washington had moved his army to the north side of the Schuylkill River, first to an encampment near Pennypacker Mills in Schwenksville, then to the Peter Wentz farmstead in Worcester, scarcely 10 miles away from the main British force. Some 9,000 redcoats were camped at Germantown, then a small village 5 miles west of Philadelphia. The British had another 3,000 soldiers stationed in Philadelphia itself.

Washington had one advantage. He knew from intercepted letters that the British had detached some of their units from Germantown to try to destroy the obstacles that were preventing British ships from reaching Philadelphia with much-needed supplies (see pages 79–83). Therefore, he reasoned, General Howe's force at Germantown had been weakened and would be more vulnerable to an attack.

Scarcely a week after the British occupied Philadelphia, Washington put his plan into action. Under cover of darkness on the night of October 3, his troops began their march toward the British encampment, following four different roads that converged on Germantown. Each of these separate forces was to time its arrival to coordinate its assault with those of the other contingents.

In spite of the careful planning, the central column arrived before the column to its left. What's more, as dawn broke on October 4, a heavy ground fog enveloped the area, making it difficult for the soldiers to see any distance. Despite having only half of his attack force at hand, Washington ordered the assault. The Continental infantrymen, among their ranks survivors of the recent defeat at Paoli, pushed the defenders back in heavy fighting. For the first time in the war, the British were forced to retreat. A British officer later wrote: "Two columns of the enemy [the Americans] had nearly got around our flank. But this was the first time we had ever retreated from the Americans and it was with great difficulty that we could get the men to obey our orders."

The steady advance of the Americans isolated a British regiment that had lost sight of its retreating colleagues in the battle fog and smoke. With nowhere else to turn, the British leader ordered his men to occupy the Chew House, also known as Cliveden, a sturdily built stone mansion that stood in the midst of the fighting. It was the home of the chief justice of the province of Pennsylvania, Benjamin Chew. About 120 British soldiers barricaded themselves in the house and slammed shut the first-floor window shutters. Sharpshooters fired from its upper windows at the passing American soldiers.

Instead of bypassing this snipers' nest, Washington decided to obliterate it with artillery fire and therefore delayed moving his army against the enemy. But the sturdy structure withstood the cannonballs. Several

Peaceful-looking today, this mansion stood in the midst of the Battle of Germantown in 1777. The British occupied Cliveden, home of Benjamin Chew, chief justice of Pennsylvania, and sharpshooters fired on the Continental Army until they retreated. A reenactment of the battle is staged at the site each October.

daring attempts by the Americans to force their way into the house or burn it down also failed.

Meanwhile, other attackers of the central column had captured Market Square, the center of the British encampment, and the British seemed to be on the run. But Washington's left column had lost its way and arrived late. One of its units mistook the firing in the vicinity of the Chew House for an enemy attack and opened fire on its own troops. This confused firing caused consternation in the American ranks and brought the advance to a halt.

When the soldiers at Market Square failed to get the support they had expected from the left column and ran low on ammunition, the assault stalled, and the British defenders recovered. At this critical juncture, the British were reinforced by troops from Philadelphia who had marched in double time the 5 miles to Germantown to get into the action.

Now the momentum of the battle shifted to the British, who forced the Americans to retreat. The sharpshooters at the Chew House, the site that proved such a stumbling block to the Americans, continued to fire at the retreating Continentals.

The Americans nevertheless managed to make an orderly with-drawal. It had been a long and terrible day. They had marched 14 miles in the predawn darkness, fought a fierce five-hour battle, and then retreated 20 miles, all in only twenty-seven hours. The troops were exhausted but far from discouraged. Most, in fact, were encouraged by the fact they had come so close to winning a pitched battle against the enemy. Had it not been for the fog, the late arrival of the left column, some poor leadership, and the lengthy attack on the Chew House, they might have won the day. Such a hard-fought defeat increased their confidence in themselves and their leaders. The army would be eager to fight again.

The official report of the 10,000 Americans engaged listed 152 killed, 521 wounded, and more than 400 missing. Of the 10,000 British engaged, more than 500 were killed, wounded, and missing.

WHAT YOU SEE TODAY

The British defensive alignment of troops at Germantown centered on what is now Market Square at the intersection of Germantown Avenue and School House Lane. In those days, the square held a market house, the town hall, a firehouse, prison, stocks, and public scales. A cannon salvaged from the British warship *Augusta*, sunk by the Americans in the nearby Delaware River during the British attack on Fort Mifflin, stands today in the square at the foot of a monument to a later war, the Civil War.

Cliveden. The home built for Pennsylvania chief justice Benjamin Chew in 1763–67 was a focal point during the battle. Members of the Chew family resided at Cliveden continuously from the 1760s until 1971. Today, the historic mansion, owned by the National Trust for Historic Preservation, displays original eighteenth- and nineteenth-century furnishings. A reenactment of the battle is held at the site on the first Saturday in October.

Germantown Historical Society. This redbrick building facing Market Square offers visitors an orientation to Germantown, the first German settlement in the New World. Its museum displays cannonballs and musket bullets from the Revolutionary War, Continental currency, and battle memorabilia. Its library reflects 300 years of local history. Open year-round Tuesday through Friday, 10 A.M. to 4 P.M.; Sunday, 1 P.M. to 5 P.M. For more information, call 215-844-1683.

Deshler-Morris House. Built by the Philadelphia merchant David Deshler in 1772, the house was used as headquarters by General Howe during the Battle of Germantown. Later, in 1792, George Washington and his family occupied the house as a summer retreat from the city while he was president. A unit of Independence National Historical Park, it is furnished with period furniture. Open April through December, Tuesday through Saturday, 1 P.M. to 4 P.M. Admission: adults $1, students 50 cents.

Grumblethorpe. Built in 1744 by John Wister. British general James Agnew made his headquarters in this home on Germantown Avenue and died there of wounds he suffered in the battle. Open Tuesday, Thursday, and Sunday, 1 P.M. to 4 P.M.

A guided walking tour that includes the Germantown Historical Society, Grumblethorpe, and the Deshler-Morris House leaves periodically from the historical society. A $9 fee for adults includes admission to the historical society museum. For more information, call 215-844-1683.

When to visit: Cliveden is open April through December, Thursday through Sunday, 12 noon to 4 P.M.

Admission fees: Adults $6.

Special events: First Saturday in October: reenactment of the Battle of Germantown; first Saturday in May: Mount Airy Day; lectures and programs.

Tours of the site: Group tours.

Time needed to visit: One hour.

Special considerations: Handicapped accessible.

Parking: Free on-street parking.

Gift shop: Books, pamphlets, and memorabilia.

Directions: From I-76 (Schuylkill Expressway), take Lincoln Drive. Go 2 miles, and turn right on Johnson Street. At the fourth traffic light, turn left on Germantown Avenue. Go one block, and turn right on Cliveden Street to reach the site.

Other nearby sites

Pennypacker Mills. Served as the site of the first encampment of Washington's troops before the Battle of Germantown (September 25–29) as well as an encampment afterward (October 5–8). The farmhouse, built in 1720 and later enlarged and occupied by a Pennsylvania governor, Samuel W. Pennypacker, was used as a headquarters by Washington. Several Revolutionary soldiers are buried on the property. The historic landscape, home, and museum are preserved as a Montgomery County historic park. Located at PA Route 73 and Haldeman Road in Schwenksville. For more information, call 215-287-9349.

Peter Wentz Farmstead. Served as the second encampment site for Washington's troops before the Battle of Germantown, as well as their encampment site immediately following the battle in October 1777. Washington and his officers planned their battle strategy at the farmhouse. The house and barn, both original structures, are preserved by Montgomery County and are open to the public as a historic park. Located off PA Route 73, south of PA Route 202 in Worcester. For more information, call 215-584-5104.

Stenton Mansion. The home of William Penn's secretary James Logan, built in 1730 on a 3-acre site. Gen. William Howe stayed here before the Battle of Germantown, then moved to the Deshler-Morris House. Open March through December, Tuesday through Saturday, 1 P.M. to 4 P.M. Located at 18th Street and Windrim Street in Germantown. For more information, call 215-329-7312.

Rittenhouse Town. One of the first paper mills in America, this Colonial industrial village encompassed more than forty structures, including a paper mill, church, school, and fire company. Seven buildings remain and can be viewed on a walking tour. An orientation film is available. A museum includes an operating diorama of the first paper mill. Located on Wissahickon Avenue, near Lincoln Drive. Open Monday through Friday, 10 A.M. to 4 P.M., Saturday and Sunday, 12 noon to 4 P.M. Admission fee.

Fort Washington State Park and Hope Lodge

WHITEMARSH SKIRMISHES

Fort Washington State Park
500 Bethlehem Pike
Fort Washington, PA 19034
215-591-5250

Hope Lodge
553 South Bethlehem Pike
Fort Washington, PA 19034
215-646-1595
fax: 215-628-9471

After the Battle of Germantown, Gen. George Washington and his troops withdrew into the countryside. But one month later, when Gen. William Howe pulled his troops back from Germantown into Philadelphia, Washington moved closer to the city again. On November 2, 1777, he established an encampment at Whitemarsh, 15 miles from the city, where he could keep a close eye on British troop movements.

At Whitemarsh, he deployed his army along a ridgeline that ran perpendicular to both Germantown Road and Bethlehem Road, the major routes from Philadelphia. The soldiers set to work building defenses on the ridgeline's three hills: Militia Hill, Fort Hill, and Camp Hill. They built redoubts and dug trenches designed to repel a British attack. Rows of abatis, pointed stakes driven at an angle into the ground, were constructed between the protective trenches. Pickets were posted at strategic intersections to warn of the enemy's approach.

Once the British had cleared the Delaware River of the obstacles placed there by the Continental forces (see pages 79–83), General Howe was free to turn his attention to the troops at Whitemarsh. On December 5, just after midnight, 10,000 British soldiers left their camps in Philadelphia and marched in two columns toward Whitemarsh. Although Washington had been forewarned of the British movement by spies in the city, the threatened attack by the redcoats was confirmed when an American patrol sighted the British marching through Germantown in the early-morning hours.

Howe observed the American defenses at Whitemarsh from a nearby church tower. He decided to use the same strategy that had served him so well at the Battle of Brandywine. He would use a portion of his troops to press forward against the center of the American defenses. Then he would direct a larger part of his force to make a long march around the right to flank the American defenses and attack them on their left, at Camp Hill.

But this time the strategy did not work. Washington became aware of Howe's tactic and shifted troops to the left side of his line. One of the defending units was Morgan's riflemen, hardy frontiersmen who had just returned from the American victory at the Battle of Saratoga. Fighting "Indian style" from tree to tree, the riflemen disrupted the British attack.

The British now sent a unit of grenadiers to test the strength of the American position. "I found the rebels . . . before and behind their strongest abatis which went up the slope of the hill," a British officer wrote. "They had dug trenches with embrasures every two or three hundreds paces." The grenadiers were turned back.

The British assault in the center fared no better. Continental soldiers repelled the attack of a force commanded by Maj. Gen. Charles Grey, the same commander who had led the bayonet-wielding attack at Paoli (see pages 75–77) two months before.

The next morning, the Americans were in line and ready to fight again, but General Howe chose not to resume the assault. He had failed to outflank the Americans, his supplies were nearly exhausted, and the nights were getting increasingly cold. Consequently, he broke off the attack, pulled his troops out of the field, and marched back to the comfort of Philadelphia.

In a later report to his superior, Howe wrote: "The Army made a movement from hence [Philadelphia] towards the Enemy posted at Whitemarsh 14 miles distant, in expectation of making an attack in some accessible Part to the strong Ground they possessed but after presenting ourselves to them for four Days in different Positions, and trying both their Flanks, their Situation was found too well secured both by Labor and Nature to make an attack advisable, therefore on the afternoon of the 8th the Army returned to the City."

Even though the Americans had successfully fought off the British, Washington realized that Whitemarsh would be difficult to defend and was too close to the British in Philadelphia. Three days later, he marched his army to the winter encampment at Valley Forge.

Hope Lodge on Bethlehem Pike was used during the Whitemarsh encampment and skirmishes as headquarters for Washington's surgeon general John Cochran of the Continental Army. Reenactors relive those Colonial days at the annual Revolutionary War Encampment.

WHAT YOU SEE TODAY

Fort Hill. This hill held part of the Continental line against attacks by the British during the fighting on December 7, 1777. A reconstructed redoubt in Fort Washington State Park marks the place where a redoubt once stood at this high point. A 300-year-old tulip poplar tree grows nearby. The park and the community of Fort Washington were named for the fortifications built here in 1777.

Militia Hill. Units of the Pennsylvania militia under Brig. Gen. John Cadwalader, Brig. Gen. William Irvine, and Maj. John Armstrong held positions along this ridge. Today visitors find an overlook and a picnic area here.

Hope Lodge. The home of William West at the time of the fighting, Hope Lodge was used as the headquarters of the surgeon general of the Continental Army, John Cochran. The West family continued to live in the house during the six-week encampment. The mansion, Georgian in architecture, was built in 1745 by a wealthy Philadelphia merchant. It has been fully restored and contains period furnishings. It is managed by the Pennsylvania Historical and Museum Commission and is the scene of annual Revolutionary War reenactments. On exhibit is an original order from General Washington to his troops directing that no trees on Mr. West's property should be cut for firewood.

Clifton House. Built in 1801, Clifton House was formerly the Sandy Run Tavern. It has twice been demolished by fire and rebuilt. Operated by the Fort Washington Historical Society, it houses a valuable library and museum of local importance and is periodically open to the public.

Mather Mill. Stone gristmill originally built by a pioneer settler about 1686 and reconstructed in 1830. It operated for two centuries, grinding corn and grain.

Emlen House. This 1745 farmhouse served as headquarters for Gen. George Washington during the Whitemarsh encampment. A council of war held here November 24, 1777, decided not to mount a second attack on British-held Philadelphia after the failure of the Battle of Germantown. Not open to the public.

When to visit: Fort Washington State Park is open year-round, 8 A.M. to sunset; Hope Lodge is open Tuesday through Saturday, 9 A.M. to 4 P.M.; Sunday, 12 noon to 4 P.M.

Admission fees: State park free; Hope Lodge, adults $3.50, seniors $3, children $1.50.

Special events: September 1 to November 30: hawk watch at Militia Hill in the state park; first weekend in November: 1777 Revolutionary War encampment at Hope Lodge.

Tours of the site: Self-guided with park folder.

Time needed to visit: Two hours.

Special considerations: Some picnic tables and restrooms handicapped accessible.

Parking: Free.

Gift shop: At Hope Lodge. Books, crafts, memorabilia.

Directions: The park and Hope Lodge lie between the towns of Fort Washington and Flourtown along Bethlehem Pike. Take exit 26 from the Pennsylvania Turnpike. To reach Hope Lodge, follow signs on Pennsylvania Avenue, then left on Bethlehem Pike. Use park entrances along Bethlehem Pike to reach Fort Hill; use entrance along Skippack Pike (PA Route 73), to reach Militia Hill.

Valley Forge National Historical Park

Box 853
Valley Forge, PA 19482-0953
610-783-1077

After the British pulled their troops back into Philadelphia follow-ing the action at Whitemarsh, the weather worsened. Washing-ton knew he needed to find a location for winter quarters where his troops could get protection against the elements and thus survive the winter.

Whitemarsh, he decided, was too close to Philadelphia. But he wanted to stay close enough to Philadelphia to inhibit British foraging expeditions and stay alert for possible surprise attacks. Also, officials of Pennsylvania were insisting that the army remain in the area to protect the farm country from the enemy. Some of his generals suggested the town of Reading; others suggested Wilmington or Bethlehem. Anthony Wayne suggested Valley Forge, 22 miles from Philadelphia. It was situ-ated in a strong defensive location and had plenty of trees that could be cut to make huts and redoubts and provide firewood.

The troops left Whitemarsh for Valley Forge on December 11. "We crossed the Schuylkill in a cold, rainy and snowy night upon a bridge of wagons set end to end and joined together by boards and planks," one soldier wrote in his diary.

When Washington's poorly fed, ill-equipped army, weary from a number of long marches, struggled into Valley Forge on December 19, winds blew as the 12,000 Continental soldiers prepared for winter's fury. Grounds for brigade encampments were selected, and trenches and redoubts were planned and begun. Within days of the army's arrival, the Schuylkill River was covered with ice and the snow was 6 inches deep.

Washington ordered that the troops be housed in huts as soon as possible and offered a $12 reward for the first well-constructed hut to be completed in each regiment. He directed that each hut was to house twelve men, and be 14 feet wide, 15 feet long, and 6½ feet high. The huts were to be erected along orderly company streets, chinked with clay, and roofed with whatever material the men could find. Each hut would have a chimney and fireplace for warmth and cooking. The first hut was reportedly finished late on December 21, and more than 800 were under construction by the end of the month.

Soldiers received irregular supplies of meat and bread, some getting their only nourishment from "firecake," a tasteless mixture of flour and water baked on a hot stone. Animals fared no better. Gen. Henry Knox, Washington's chief of artillery, wrote that hundreds of horses either starved to death or died of exhaustion.

There was no meat available and only twenty-five barrels of flour. Things were so bad that Washington was genuinely concerned that "this Army must inevitably . . . starve, dissolve or disperse." Repeated appeals to the national and state legislatures brought only sporadic supplies or provisions, barely enough to keep the troops alive. The men were supposed to receive a daily allowance of a pound of meat or fish but were sometimes lucky to get that much in a week. Many resorted to hunting local small game, such as squirrels, rabbits, and raccoons. The meat shortage did not begin to ease until spring and was not eliminated until the migrating shad came up the Schuylkill River in April.

Clothing, too, was inadequate. The ceaseless marching had worn out many of the soldiers' shoes. Blankets were scarce. Tattered garments were seldom replaced. At one point, these shortages caused nearly 4,000 men to be listed as unfit for duty.

Undernourished and poorly clothed, living in crowded, damp quarters, the men were beset by sickness and disease. Typhus, typhoid, dysentery, and pneumonia killed as many as 3,000 that winter. Although Washington repeatedly petitioned for relief, Congress was unable to provide it, and the soldiers continued to suffer. Women relatives of some of the enlisted men alleviated some of the suffering by providing valuable services such as laundry and nursing.

"It is more alarming than you will probably conceive," Washington wrote to New York governor George Clinton. "For some days past, there has been little less than a famine in camp. A part of the army has been a week without any kind of flesh, and the rest three or four days. Naked and starving as they are, we cannot enough admire the incomparable patience and fidelity of the soldiery that they have not been ere this excited by their sufferings to a general mutiny and dispersion."

Despite these conditions, the army managed to endure—much to the amazement of its officers. Supplies began to arrive more regularly

NATIONAL PARK SERVICE, RICHARD FREAR

Soldiers warm themselves as they cook their evening meal in front of a fire during a reenactment of their wintertime encampment at Valley Forge National Historical Park.

when Maj. Gen. Nathanael Greene took over the quartermaster department in March.

Their commander had much to endure as well. Besides being concerned over his troops' well-being, Washington at this period had to contend with the jealous criticism and intrigues of fellow officers who sought to have him replaced. Letters went back and forth between disloyal officers, disparaging Washington's military talents. But the conspiracy finally dissolved, and Maj. Gen. Thomas Conway, its instigator, resigned.

Meanwhile Washington was also encouraging professionalism among his troops. Here he got a tremendous boost from a portly Prussian officer who offered to help the Continental Army—Baron Friedrich von Steuben, to whom was given the task of developing and carrying out an effective training program to upgrade the military efficiency of the troops. The army's greatest fault was a lack of organization and drill at the most basic level. Low-ranking officers and the non-commissioned officers, the backbone of any army, knew little about military duties and procedures, and the troops did not know how to move or march in the field. Most of them had come from farm or frontier and had little military training. This skilled drillmaster, recently arrived from Europe, tirelessly drilled the regiments into an effective fighting force.

The baron set down a simplified field manual based on the Prussian system and written in French, for von Steuben knew little English. His bilingual aide, John Laurens, and Capt. Alexander Hamilton translated the manual into English, and copies were handwritten and distributed to each company.

Von Steuben shocked many American officers by breaking tradition to work directly with the men. From dawn to dusk, his familiar voice was heard in camp above the sounds of marching men and shouted commands. Soon companies, regiments, then brigades moved smartly from line to column, column to line, loaded muskets with precision, and drove imaginary redcoats from the field by skillful charges with the bayonet.

As the weeks went by, the army under Washington's persistent leadership underwent a dramatic transformation. Slowly but steadily, the endurance, bravery, and sacrifice of the soldiers began to pay off. Increasing amounts of supplies and equipment began to reach the camp. New recruits arrived. Spring brought word that France had allied itself with the Americans against their old foe. This meant that more supplies and munitions would be coming to the hard-pressed Americans, and the French fleet would do battle with the British fleet. At Valley Forge, the welcome news of the French alliance was celebrated with a grand review of the troops, an artillery salute, and the firing of muskets.

Now Washington wanted to know what the British intentions were. To find out, he dispatched General Lafayette with 2,000 men to cross the Schuylkill River and reconnoiter close to the British lines. But the British, tipped off by a spy, nearly surrounded Lafayette's force with 16,000 men at Barren Hill. Only by faking a counterattack and using a little-known escape route was Lafayette able to extricate his men, recross the river, and return safely to Valley Forge.

In June, word came that the British had marched out of Philadelphia and were moving toward New York. On June 19, 1778, six months after its arrival, the Continental Army marched away from

Valley Forge in pursuit of the redcoats. It was a rejuvenated army, a strong, dependable force that had been steeled by a winter of privation.

WHAT YOU SEE TODAY

Visitors Center. Built during the Bicentennial of the American Revolution in 1976, the visitors center houses a collection of eighteenth-century arms and an original marquee tent used by General Washington in the field. Park interpreters familiarize visitors with special events, seasonal programs, and historic sites within the park. An orientation film is shown.

Soldiers' Huts. Reconstructed log huts similar to the ones built by the soldiers in 1777–78 are located at several places in the park, at the sites where they originally stood. Visitors may step into a hut to get a sense of the soldiers' living conditions. Living-history demonstrations are occasionally held at the Muhlenberg hut area. Two reconstructed redoubts illustrate the defensive measures used to protect Valley Forge against attack.

Washington's Headquarters. Visitors may tour the stone house Washington used for his headquarters, a home once owned by Isaac Potts, ironmaster at Valley Forge, the iron forge along Valley Creek that had been destroyed by the British prior to the encampment. It is furnished much the way it was when Washington resided here. Washington lived in a large tent until he could occupy the house. Nearby are replica huts that housed the commander in chief's lifeguards. During the encampment, Martha Washington joined her husband here for four months.

Varnum's Quarters. This early-eighteenth-century farmhouse, which overlooks the Grand Parade, served as quarters for Brig. Gen. James Varnum of Rhode Island. Nearby stands a statue of Maj. Gen. Friedrich von Steuben, who supervised the training of the Continental Army.

Artillery Park. A number of eighteenth-century cannons are grouped here, where Maj. Gen. Henry Knox concentrated his artillery.

Memorial Arch. The National Memorial Arch, a dominant feature of the park, was dedicated in 1917 and commemorates the "patience and fidelity" of the soldiers who wintered at Valley Forge. Lighted at night, the arch is the site of occasional commemorative events.

Washington Memorial Chapel and Valley Forge Historical Society Museum. Visitors are welcome to visit the chapel, an active Episcopal church located on private property within the park. A carillon in the chapel tower provides concerts on summer evenings. In the same building complex, the Valley Forge Historical Museum displays artifacts representing the social, political, military, and symbolic aspects of Valley Forge and the Revolutionary War. An admission fee is charged.

When to visit: Park open daily, except Christmas and New Year's Day; Washington's Headquarters and visitors center open 9 A.M. to 5 P.M.

Admission fees: $2 per person (over sixteen) to tour Washington's Headquarters.

Special events: December 19: march-in of Washington's army; February: Washington's birthday celebration; May 6: French Alliance Day; June 19: March-out of Washington's army.

Tours of the site: Self-guided. Auto tape narrations may be rented at the visitors center.

Time needed to visit: Three hours.

Parking: Free.

Gift shop: Books, booklets, maps, and videos.

Directions: Park is 20 miles west of Philadelphia. Entrances from major highways are well marked. If traveling on the Pennsylvania Turnpike, take Valley Forge exit 24 and follow signs to the park. PA Route 23 runs through the park.

Tourist information

Valley Forge Convention and Visitor Bureau, 600 West Germantown Pike, Plymouth Meeting, PA 19462, telephone 610-834-1550.

Valley Forge Tourist Information Center, Valley Forge National Historical Park, telephone 610-783-1077. Both centers may be reached by calling 888-VisitVF or visiting the website www.valleyforge.org.

Other nearby sites

Montgomery Cemetery. The final resting place for four Pennsylvania Civil War generals: Adam Slemmer, Samuel K. Zook, Winfield Scott Hancock, and John F. Hartranft. Slemmer commanded Fort Pickens at the start of the Civil War; Zook, a brigade commander, was killed at Gettysburg; Hancock commanded the 2nd Corps of the Potomac at Gettysburg and later was a presidential candidate; Hartranft commanded two Norristown-based regiments and later became a governor of Pennsylvania. Located just off Main Street in Norristown on a bluff overlooking the Schuylkill River.

Hopewell Furnace National Historic Site. Built by Mark Bird in 1770, this site is typical of many iron-making communities that manufactured tools, horseshoes, and cannonballs. The ironmaster's house, along with a 32-foot high furnace stack, water wheel, charcoal shed, blacksmith shop and tenant cottages are open to the public year-round. Located 6 miles south of Birdsboro, PA, on Route 345 in Elverson. For more information, call 610-582-8773.

Mill Grove and Audubon Wildlife Sanctuary. The American home of naturalist John James Audubon from 1803 to 1806, now a museum that features paintings by Audubon and displays about his life. Numerous trails wind through the 175-acre nature preserve. Located on Pawlings Road in Audubon, across the river from Valley Forge, Mill Grove is a Montgomery County historic park and a National Historic Landmark. Open Tuesday through Sunday. For more information, call 610-666-5593.

Pottsgrove Manor. The 1752 Georgian manor house of wealthy ironmaster John Potts, founder of Pottstown, is located on West King Street in Pottstown. Open Thursday through Sunday. For information, call 610-326-4014.

LANDMARKS
OF
OTHER EARLY
CONFLICTS

Bushy Run Battlefield

PONTIAC'S REBELLION

Route 993
Jeannette, PA 15644
724-527-5584
fax: 412-527-5610
e-mail: bushyrun@westol.com

After the French had been pushed out of their forts along the Allegheny River—Fort Duquesne, Fort Machault, Fort Presque Isle, and other smaller forts—in 1758, the British gained uncontested control of western Pennsylvania. With the fall of Quebec in 1759 and Montreal in 1760, and finally the formal surrender of New France to the British, Great Britain became the sole Colonial power in the region.

But Britain's dominance came as bitter news to the American Indians, who had long had a mutually beneficial working arrangement with the French trappers and traders, dating back to the early forays of the French *voyageurs*. The Indians sold furs, food, and supplies to these French traders; from them they obtained in exchange muskets, gunpowder, shot, iron implements, and liquor. Now this two-way barter system was disrupted.

Furthermore, the British failed to honor the treaty they had made with the Indians to keep Europeans from occupying their lands in western Pennsylvania. Instead of giving up the former French forts they had conquered, the British strengthened them. And instead of presenting the Indians with gifts, as the French had done, they treated them harshly. At major trading posts such as Detroit, Michilimackinac, Niagara, and Pitt, the Indians were denied the powder, lead, and alcohol that had contributed to their friendship with the French. They also suffered from the ravages of smallpox, which had been spread across the ocean by the settlers.

By 1763, many Indian leaders saw the British as a threat to their way of life. The Iroquois, long the dominant Indian confederation in the East, began to circulate wampum belts—a signal for war—in the West to enlist allies for the probable day of conflict. An Ottawa war chief, Pontiac, watched the encroachment by the settlers upon Indian

Many Indians like this one displayed at the Bushy Run Museum fought with the British wearing black and red body paint, which they believed enhanced their ferocity. They wore only breechcloths, moccasins, and leather leggings for protection from the woods and attacked with tomahawks and muskets they had bought from the French.

lands and perceived the threat. He was influenced by an Indian spiritual leader, Neolin, who encouraged the Indians to repudiate the white man's ways and instead to adopt the traditional native ways. Neolin also predicted the imminent destruction of the European race.

For months, Pontiac worked to organize the various staunchly independent tribes into a united opposition against the British. Finally he negotiated agreement among most of the tribes of the Midwest to mount a coordinated attack on Fort Detroit on the shore of Lake Michigan. This act of defiance in turn helped ignite the fire of resistance that would soon envelop the frontier.

Other tribes now attacked British forts and settlements throughout what was then known as the Northwest Territory. In June, Fort LeBoeuf, Fort Venango (formerly Fort Machault), and Fort Presque Isle, all on the Allegheny River in western Pennsylvania, fell to the attacking Indians.

Fort Ligonier was attacked but held out against capture. Fort Bedford was not attacked, but its lines of communication were cut. Warriors from at least four tribes—the Delaware, Mingo, Shawnee, and Wyandot—surrounded and besieged Fort Pitt.

Within two months, Pontiac's uprising had resulted in the capture of nine forts, forced a tenth to be abandoned, and laid siege to strongly fortified Fort Detroit and Fort Pitt. War parties severed lines of communication between frontier forts and nearby settlements and drove hundreds of settlers from their homes and farms. As a result of these actions, the Indians neutralized British power in the region and temporarily gained control of much of the frontier stretching from Pennsylvania to present-day Michigan.

Back at his headquarters in New York, the British military commander for the colonies, Gen. Jeffrey Amherst, was angered and ordered the extirpation of the rebelling "savages." He called on Col. Henry Bouquet, the astute Swiss mercenary who had so skillfully executed the plan to capture Fort Duquesne and oust the French from the Allegheny River Valley. Bouquet's new orders were to organize an expedition to reinforce and supply the threatened Fort Pitt.

Mobilizing his troops at Carlisle, Bouquet organized two regiments of battle-tested Scottish Highlanders, one regiment of newly recruited American settlers known as the 60th Royal Americans, and a handful of savvy frontier woodsmen and scouts. With a force of 450, he marched 70 miles to Fort Bedford, then on another 60 miles to Fort Ligonier. Anxious to push his men on to the beleaguered Fort Pitt, he unloaded all his wagons and shifted his bags of flour and other supplies to 330 horses to undertake the last part of the journey, 50 miles over the steep Allegheny Mountains. Little did he realize the important role these flour bags would later play.

Unknown to Bouquet, the Indians besieging Fort Pitt had received word that he was headed west with a large force. They foresaw a great opportunity—to ambush the approaching British troops, prevent the reinforcement of Fort Pitt, and win a great victory. So they pulled their warriors from the siege of the fort and moved east to meet the approaching English force.

On August 5, Bouquet and his expedition had approached within 25 miles of Fort Pitt. That day they had marched 17 miles, it was hot, and the men needed to refill their canteens. As the soldiers made their way toward a creek called Bushy Run, the Indian force suddenly attacked.

Bouquet himself later described how difficult it was for his vulnerable British soldiers to combat the hit-and-run tactics of the Indians. "As soon as they [the Indians] were driven from one post, they appeared on another till by continued reinforcement they were able to at last surround us, and attacked the convoy left in our rear, thus obliging us to march back to protect it. The action then became general."

By the time darkness fell, Bouquet's force had lost fifty men killed or wounded and had been forced to retreat to a hilltop, where they established a defensive perimeter that included a circle of flour bags.

The Battle of Bushy Run was fought around the "Flour Bag Fort," which protected the wounded on Edge Hill, as depicted by these reenactors. The 42nd and 77th Royal Highlanders and 60th Royal Americans were under the leadership of Col. Henry Bouquet. Today a slice of Ligonier blue rock marks the site.

The wounded were placed behind this "Flour Bag Fort," while able-bodied defenders fired over them at the attacking Indians. The attack waned as night fell.

Bouquet was doubtful his force could overcome the Indians the next day. "In case of another engagement," he wrote in his journal, "I fear insurmountable difficulties . . . being already so much weakened by the losses of this day in men and horses besides the additional necessity of carrying the wounded. . . . The want of water is much more intolerable than the enemy's fire."

Sure enough, at daylight on August 6, the Indian warriors resumed the attack. The British were exhausted not only from the previous day's fighting, also but from their strenuous march into the wilderness. They were also suffering from thirst on this hot summer day, as the Indian attack had prevented them from replenishing their water supply at the stream.

In desperation, Bouquet devised a plan to fool the Indians into believing that part of his remaining force had left. By this stratagem, he hoped to draw the Indians from the protective cover of the forest into the open, where they would be better targets.

Bouquet tells it this way: "The barbarians, mistaking these motions for a retreat, hurried headlong on . . . but at the very moment that [they were] certain of success . . . two companies sallied forth out from a part of the hill they could not observe and fell upon their right flank." With bayonets fixed, the soldiers charged the Indians.

Indians feared the bayonets. This sudden charge from the flank surprised them, and they fled the field, losing some sixty men in the fighting. Thus ended the battle. "We pursued them till they were totally dispersed," Bouquet reported. The Indians dissolved into the forest.

The British had lost 115 men killed, wounded, or missing. The Indians lost an estimated 50 or 60. The battle became a crucial turning point of Pontiac's War. The British had saved Fort Pitt from capture and restored their lines of communication. The major Indian threat to the frontier had been repelled, although sporadic attacks continued. A year later, Bouquet led another expedition to the Muskingum River in Ohio, where he met with the remnants of the Delaware and Shawnee nations. He persuaded them to negotiate a peace treaty and arranged for the release of hundreds of white hostages the Indians had captured.

WHAT YOU SEE TODAY

Battle Monument. A granite slab surrounded by stacked concrete "bags" marks the location of the "Flour Bag Fort," the defensive position improvised by the soldiers at the Battle of Bushy Run. On the plaque attached to the slab are inscribed the words of Col. Henry Bouquet describing the desperate battle and showing a diagram of the action.

Soldiers' Graves. A marker atop a nearby hill commemorates the unmarked graves of fifty soldiers killed in the battle. Two flags fly over the grave site.

Visitors Center. The exhibits use interactive technology, including a video based on the letters of Colonel Bouquet, a fiber-optic map that explains his strategy, artifacts, mannequins, and photographs. Visitors can try on pieces of a soldier's uniform.

When to visit: Wednesday to Sunday, 9 A.M. to 5 P.M. Visitors center is open April 1 to October 31, Wednesday to Saturday, 9 A.M. to 5 P.M., and Sunday, 12noon to 5 P.M.

Admission fees: Adults $2, seniors $1.50, children $1.

Special events: First full weekend in August: anniversary reenactment of the Battle of Bushy Run, with Indian and British reenactors each living in a separate encampment and staging a mock battle. Educational programs and lectures held throughout the year.

Tours of the site: Three self-guided trails lead past the critical sites of the two-day battle. Group tours also available.

Time needed to visit: Two hours.

Special considerations: Handicapped accessible.

Parking: Free on-site parking.

Gift shop: Books, reproductions, historical prints, and toys.

Directions: From the east, take Pennsylvania Turnpike to exit 8, New Stanton–Greensburg. Follow U.S. Route 119 North to PA Route 66 North (a toll road). Take PA Route 66 North to the Greensburg–Harrison City exit. Turn left off the exit ramp onto Old Route 66, and head north to PA Route 993 West. Go 3 miles to Bushy Run Battlefield.

Tourist information

Laurel Highlands Visitors Bureau, 120 East Main Street, Ligonier, PA 15658, telephone 724-238-5661, website www.laurelhighlands.org.

Other nearby sites.

Historic Hanna's Town. This town grew up around Robert Hanna's Tavern and became the county seat for southwestern Pennsylvania. In 1775, the citizens made a stand for independence by adopting Hanna's Town Resolves, and raised a battalion to fight in the Revolution. On July 3, 1782, a party of Indians and British rangers from Canada burned the town and took captives back to Canada. Located 3 miles north of Greensburg between Routes 119 and 819, the settlement has been reconstructed and is administered by the Westmoreland County Historical Society. For more information, call 724-836-1800.

Path of Progress. A 500-mile-long route of 21 tourist locations, including forts, battlefields, rural settlements, canals, iron and steel mills, a railroad museum, coal mines, and the Johnstown Flood National Memorial. For further information write the Southwestern Pennsylvania Heritage Preservation Commission, P. O. Box 565, Hollidaysburg 16648 or call 814-696-9380.

Wyoming Historical
and Geological Society

YANKEE-PENNAMITE WARS

49 South Franklin Street
Wilkes-Barre, PA 18701
570-823-6244
fax: 570-823-9011

The foundation for a land dispute between Yankee settlers from Connecticut and settlers from Pennsylvania was laid by conflicting grants of land in the New World that were awarded by an English king. In 1662, King Charles II granted to the colony of Connecticut in North America lands that extended southward to the 41st degree of latitude, or about to the midpoint of present-day Pennsylvania. Nineteen years later, in 1681, the same king absentmindedly granted to William Penn and his Quakers land that extended northward to the 42nd degree of latitude, thus overlapping the Connecticut grant. It did not help that these land grants presumably stretched all the way west to the Pacific Ocean.

In 1750, a group of Connecticut explorers discovered the fertile Wyoming Valley, a region that stretches along the northern reaches of the Susquehanna River where it flows past today's Wilkes-Barre. The Wyoming Valley gets its name from an Iroquois Indian word meaning "wide plain." Citing the land grant from King Charles II, Connecticut entrepreneurs formed the Susquehanna Company and in 1754 negotiated a "purchase" of land from Indians of the Onondaga Council, whom they reputedly plied with liquor and persuaded to put their marks on a document of sale. When the Pennsylvanians heard of this transaction, they immediately protested this "unlawful" action by the "Yankee intruders."

As a result of the "purchase," a few Connecticut settlers soon moved into the valley, but they were driven out in 1763 when widespread Indian raids generated by Pontiac's Rebellion swept eastward across Pennsylvania and into the Wyoming Valley (see pages 103–7). When the Indian uprising was finally quelled, several hundred more Connecticut families moved into the valley. The Penn family, proprietors of Pennsylvania, once again protested this immigration of New

Englanders and in 1763 obtained a British court order requiring Connecticut to stop further incursions of their people into the disputed territory. Furthermore, in 1768, the Penns, in the Treaty of Fort Stanwix, persuaded the Iroquois to repudiate their 1754 sale of the Wyoming Valley land to the Susquehanna Company, thus depriving the Yankees of this justification for settling in the valley.

Undeterred, however, the Susquehanna Company surveyed five townships in the vicinity of the present city of Wilkes-Barre, offering a plot 5 miles square to any group of forty Connecticut settlers who would move to the valley and promise to defend their land against any Pennsylvania claimants. The first settlers from Connecticut to migrate established a community they appropriately called Forty Fort in February 1769 (see pages 113–15). About the same time, the Penns made land grants in the same area to Pennsylvanians on the condition that they physically occupy their land and defend their property against any Connecticut claimants. These opposing land grants planted the seeds for the Yankee-Pennamite Wars.

Hostilities broke out in 1769 when 240 Connecticut men captured a blockhouse built and garrisoned by Pennsylvanians. Earlier, a Pennsylvania sheriff had lured the Yankees from their fort by deception, then arrested them and sent them to jail. More Connecticut men moved in and built a second blockhouse, but the Pennsylvanians broke down its doors, arrested thirty men, and sent them to jail too. In response, 200 more Connecticut men, led by Maj. John Durkee, president of the Susquehanna Company, arrived and this time overcame the Pennsylvanians. They laid out a town they called Wilkes-Barre, named after two members of the British Parliament who championed the colonists' desire for self-government. They built a new fort, a stockade surrounding log cabins, to house their families and named it Fort Durkee for their leader.

Spurning any compromise with the New Englanders, Gov. Thomas Penn sent out an armed force under the command of Amos Ogden, armed with a 6-pounder cannon, which captured Fort Durkee. Colonel Durkee, who earlier had been captured, then released from prison, rallied another force of Connecticut fighters. This time the New Englanders, in a surprise attack, captured the cannon and burned the fort to the ground.

Later in 1769, Capt. Amos Ogden with 140 Pennsylvanians recaptured the rebuilt Fort Durkee, plundered settlers' houses, and chased the Yankees from the valley. In December of that same year, a Connecticut force attacked once more and recaptured Fort Durkee. The

Pennsylvanians attacked again the following month, this time capturing Colonel Durkee and regaining possession of the fort.

In the summer of 1771, Capt. Zebulon Butler and seventy men from Connecticut captured a new blockhouse the Pennsylvanians had built, this one called Fort Wyoming. This time a counterattack by the Pennsylvanians failed, and they were forced to retire from the valley under an armistice.

With this battle action, the New Englanders gained control of the valley. Now more Connecticut settlers moved in to establish farms. The government of Connecticut formally recognized the Wyoming settlements, incorporating them into the new Westmoreland County. The settlers liked the Connecticut system of allocating land, in which the occupants were allowed to buy the title to their land rather than lease it, as the Pennsylvanians required. However, when the New Englanders organized yet another new town, called Muncy, the Yankee-Pennamite Wars broke out anew. Armed hostilities lasted from 1775 into the early years of the Revolution. By this time, about 5,000 people from Connecticut were living in the Wyoming Valley.

Finally, when the men from both of the contending colonies were forced to fight side by side in the Revolutionary War, the Yankee-Pennamite battles dissolved. Soon after the end of the Revolutionary War and the establishment of the U.S. government under the Articles of Confederation, Pennsylvania appealed to Congress to settle this long-standing land dispute with Connecticut. A special commission heard arguments and on December 30, 1782, issued the Trenton Decree, which rejected the Connecticut claims and confirmed Pennsylvania's possession of the region. The decree provided, however, that Pennsylvania should respect the land titles of all of the Connecticut settlers, who would be allowed to continue to live in the valley .

This proved easier to promise than to implement. More hostilities developed over the conflicting titles of the various Pennsylvania and Connecticut settlers. The controversy was not finally settled until 1807, when the Yankee-Pennamite Wars finally came to an end after four decades of intermittent fighting. A statute confirmed existing Connecticut land titles and reimbursed Pennsylvania claimants in cash for their loss of certain lands.

WHAT YOU SEE TODAY

Wyoming Historical and Geological Society. The society's headquarters contain an extensive library of reference books on the Yankee-Pennamite Wars and the Battle of Wyoming Valley, as well as a museum at 69 South Franklin Street that interprets the history of Luzerne County and its environs. Visitors can get information from the staff on local battle sites and historic sites. Open Tuesday through Friday, 12 noon to 4 P.M.; Saturday, 10 A.M. to 4 P.M.

River Common. In this 35-acre park bordering the Susquehanna River in Wilkes-Barre and adjacent to Wilkes University stand two historical markers, one identifying the site of Fort Durkee, built by the Connecticut settlers in 1769, and the other the site of Fort Wyoming, constructed by the Pennsylvania settlers in 1771 and later seized by the New Englanders. In 1779, a year after the defeat of the American defenders across the river at nearby Forty Fort in the Battle of Wyoming Valley, the troops of Maj. Gen. John Sullivan encamped at this location in preparation to march against the Iroquois to the north in a reprisal for the Wyoming Valley massacre.

Public Square. The square was laid out in 1770 by Connecticut settlers as part of the original plan for the new town of Wilkes-Barre. Located where Market Street and Main Street intersect in the heart of the city, it remains today the center of civic activities. A commemorative marker in the square identifies the site of a later fort, Fort Wilkes-Barre (1778), a stockade that was surrendered to the British after the Battle of Wyoming Valley.

When to visit: Tuesday through Friday, 12 noon to 4 P.M.; Saturday, 10 A.M. to 4 P.M.

Admission fees: Adults $5, children $1.

Special events: Occasional reenactments of the Battle of Wyoming Valley, lectures, film series, and demonstrations.

Tours of the site: Self-guided.

Time needed to visit: One hour.

Special considerations: Not handicapped accessible.

Parking: On-street metered parking.

Gift shop: Books, pamphlets, and memorabilia.

Directions: The society is located at 49 South Franklin Street in downtown Wilkes-Barre, and the museum is at 69 South Franklin Street, behind the Osterhout Free Library.

Tourist information

Luzerne County Tourist Promotion Agency, 56 Public Square in Wilkes-Barre, telephone 888-905-2872, fax 570-819-1882, website www.tourpa.com., e-mail tournepa@tournepa.com.

Wyoming Battle Monument

BATTLE OF WYOMING VALLEY

U.S. Route 11
Forty Fort, PA 18704

Wyoming Historical and Geological Society
49 South Franklin Street
Wilkes-Barre, PA 18701
570-823-6244
fax: 570-823-9011

While battles were being fought during the Revolutionary War between American forces and the British Army along the coastal plain in the East, an independent theater of guerrilla warfare existed in northwestern New York and northern Pennsylvania. Here was a war of neighbor against neighbor, cousin against cousin, as Tories, Americans who remained loyal to the Crown, fought other Americans who supported the rebel or patriot cause. In this struggle, the Six Nations of the Iroquois allied with the British, because the Indians opposed the American settlers who had dispossessed them of their lands.

In 1778, the British put together a force of 400 Tory American soldiers and 500 Iroquois at Fort Niagara, their major base on Lake Ontario. This force marched south, attacking the farmhouses of white settlers, wreaking vengeance, and gathering a rich haul of plunder. As an incentive, the British paid Indian warriors a bounty for each American scalp they took. Reprisals were as savage as the raids that had provoked them. Settlers were murdered in their beds, frontier cabins and lean-tos put to the torch, children abducted.

The most devastating of the combined British and Indian raids were directed at sites along the Susquehanna River in the Wyoming Valley, in the vicinity of present-day Wilkes-Barre. Most of the valley's settlers were strong patriots. The able-bodied men of the area had earlier enlisted in the Continental Army and were away from home with Washington's forces. That left Col. Zebulon Butler to defend the Wyoming Valley settlements with only 300 boys and old men plus a small group of rangers. They mobilized at a frontier fort named Forty Fort, the stockade that had been built to protect the first forty permanent settlers in the valley during the Yankee-Pennamite Wars.

113

The 1,200 British-led Tories and Indians struck on June 28, burning a mill and taking three prisoners, whom they later murdered. Two nearby private forts surrendered when they were threatened by the invaders. But the 300 defenders of Forty Fort sent word that they would "never give [the fort] over to the Tories and savages but stand it out to the last and defend it to the last extremity."

The Tories and Indians surrounded the fort and waited. After several days, the Tory commander, Maj. John Butler (no relation to the colonel), set fire to one of the private forts to give the impression that he and his men were retreating. It was a ruse—the Indians remained concealed in the nearby woods. But Colonel Butler and the rangers took the bait. The defenders left the protection of their fort and took off in pursuit of the raiders. Then the waiting Tories and Indians sprang the trap. At first the patriots held their ground, but once they had fired their muskets and began to reload, the Indians rushed at them with spears and tomahawks, and the inexperienced defenders turned and fled for their lives. Many of them jumped into the Susquehanna River to escape, but the Indians overtook them and killed them in the water.

More than sixty of the defenders were slaughtered. A Tory settler who lived nearby reported that he saw prisoners "tied to small trees and burnt the evening of the same day." Witnesses reported other atrocities. At dark, it was said, prisoners who had survived were chased, naked, through the campfires until they dropped from exhaustion. The raiders sustained only one Indian killed and two soldiers wounded.

The invaders swept through the valley, killing 109 other settlers and confiscating all horses and livestock. In all, 1,000 houses and countless barns and mills went up in flames. Wilkes-Barre was completely razed. Other inhabitants were either captured by the Indians or left to die of exposure in the nearby mountains.

The Wyoming Valley massacre became a symbol of Tory and Indian brutality. The Tories, expressing their outrage at the actions of the American patriots, who were resisting the authority of the mother country, often paid little attention to the accepted European rules of warfare. They neither gave nor expected mercy. When this vengeful spirit was combined with the Indian concept of unrestrained warfare, the results—as in the Battle of Wyoming Valley—were grim.

A year later, a strong American force of 1,400 under Maj. Gen. John Sullivan marched north through Wilkes-Barre and on into New York "to visit upon them [the Iroquois and allied Indian tribes] the vengeance which their cruelties deserve." The Continental soldiers set fire to Indian villages and destroyed cornfields, gardens, and orchards. In all, forty Indian villages were wiped out in the Iroquois's western New York homeland. As a result, the once powerful Iroquois Confederacy was forever crushed.

WHAT YOU SEE TODAY

Wyoming Battle Monument. This 62-foot-tall obelisk stands in a roadside park on U.S. Route 11, 1 mile north of the town of Forty Fort in Wyoming Borough. It commemorates the 179 American soldiers and settlers who were killed in the Battle of Wyoming Valley and in the massacre that followed. The remains of many of those killed are buried in a vault in the base of the monument, which stands at the site of the battle. The names of all who died are engraved on tablets around the monument's base.

Swetland Homestead. The house, whose original section dates to 1803, was built by Luke Swetland, a settler from Connecticut who was in the fort at Forty Fort during the Battle of Wyoming Valley. He was later captured by Indian attackers but escaped a year later and returned with Gen. John Sullivan's forces to reclaim his home. Visitors see period rooms that reflect the years 1803 to 1865. The homestead, listed on the National Register of Historic Places, has been restored by the Wyoming Historical and Geological Society of Wilkes-

Visitors will easily spot the 62-foot Wyoming Battle Monument as they drive along U.S. Route 11 in Forty Fort. Here British-led Tories and Indians killed 179 local militiamen and settlers, many of whom lie buried beneath the monument.

The restored house of Nathan Denison, one of the first forty migrants from Connecticut to settle in the Wyoming Valley, was built in 1790. Michael Bertheaud of the Wyoming Historical and Geological Society (left) explains to the author that it was Denison who negotiated the surrender of Forty Fort to the British forces in 1778 as the Revolutionary War swept through the valley.

Barre. Candlelight tours are conducted each December, and occasional encampments are held at the site. The Swetland Homestead is located on U.S. Route 11, .25 mile south of the Wyoming Battle Monument. Open Saturdays from Memorial Day weekend to the last Saturday before Christmas.

Nathan Denison House. This restored home, considered the oldest frame dwelling in the Wyoming Valley, was built in 1790 by Nathan Denison, one of the first forty permanent settlers, who came from Connecticut in 1769. He built the house on Abrams Creek, a tributary of the Susquehanna River. Colonel Denison was the second in command and negotiated the surrender of Forty Fort in 1778. The house is furnished with eighteenth-century antiques. Special events and programs of historical interest are presented throughout the year, and costumed interpreters greet visitors on Sunday afternoons, May through August,

1 P.M. to 4 P.M. Preserved by the Pennsylvania Historical and Museum Commission, the house is located just off U.S. Route 11 in Forty Fort at 35 Denison Street. Admission is $2 for adults.

Forty Fort Meeting House and Cemetery. The cemetery contains the graves of many of the early Connecticut settlers and their families. It is located at the corner of U.S. Route 11 and River Street in Forty Fort.

Tours of the site: Self-guided.
Time needed to visit: Half hour.
Parking: Free on street.
Directions: From downtown Wilkes-Barre take PA Route 309 west to exit 5; go north on U.S. Route 11 through Forty Fort to monument on the right.

Tourist information
Luzerne County Tourist Promotion Agency, 56 Public Square in Wilkes-Barre, telephone 888-905-2872, fax 570-819-1882, website www.tourpa.com., e-mail tournepa@tournepa.com.

Other nearby sites.
French Azilum. A refuge established by French nobility for Marie Antoinette, who was planning to come to Pennsylvania but instead was executed. It was founded in 1793 and contained about fifty log buildings and an impressive *Grand Maison* on a 300-acre site. After Napoleon pardoned those who fled the French Revolution, many of the noblemen who came to Azilum returned to France. Today you see five reconstructed log cabins, a video about the site's history, a library, and a museum. Located off U.S. Route 6 between Wyalusing and Towanda, the site is open for tours during summer months, Wednesday to Sunday, and on weekends in May, September, and October. For further information, call 570-265-3376.

Lackawanna Heritage Valley. One of the state's nine heritage regions, Lackawanna is dominated by one resource—anthracite coal. Eighty percent of the world's supply of hard coal comes from this valley, but the anthracite story is also the story of thousands of immigrants, railroading, and a natural and cultural landscape. Phone 800-229-3526 for more information.

David Bradford House

WHISKEY REBELLION

175 South Main Street
Box 537
Washington, PA 15301
724-222-3604
website: www.bradfordhouse.org

The year was 1791. It had been a decade since the American Revolution had come to an end with the British surrender at Yorktown and barely four years since the adoption of the federal Constitution for the new United States of America.

The new nation was feeling its way toward governing itself, not as a loose confederation of states, but as a federal system with a centralized national government. The new federal government had assumed many of the debts that had been incurred by the individual states in the course of fighting the Revolutionary War, but now it needed to find a way to pay this "national debt."

At the urging of Secretary of the Treasury Alexander Hamilton, Congress in March 1791 passed an act that imposed an excise tax of 25 percent on the sale of the whiskey produced by all the distillers of the country. The trouble was that most of the distillers were located in the Appalachian regions of Pennsylvania, Virginia, the Carolinas, Tennessee, and Kentucky where farmers grew rye and wheat and distilled the grain into whiskey. For many of these frontiersmen, whiskey was their main cash crop, easy to transport to a ready market in the South or to the eastern seaboard.

Moreover, whiskey in the eighteenth century was far from a luxury item. It was consumed on frequent occasions, both social and political. It was used for medicinal purposes, as freely as aspirin is today. It was touted for fevers, ague, and snakebites. Every soldier on duty got a daily ration of whiskey.

This stiff tax on whiskey at its source, therefore, hit the frontier farmers hard. There wasn't enough cash for the necessities of life, they protested, let alone for this "obnoxious tax." The tax, they argued, completely disrupted their frontier farm economy just as it was emerging commercially. And it struck hardest in the western frontier country, where whiskey was distilled, rather than in the more settled areas of the country, where it was consumed.

This excise tax came on top of several other long-standing grievances of the western settlers. The federal government, they felt, had done little to protect them from Indian raids, which had left numerous frontier families murdered or kidnapped. Neither had their government succeeded in opening up the Mississippi River system, controlled by Spain at New Orleans, so they could ship their produce down the river to market. What's more, those on the frontier resented the fact that absentee landlords, such as George Washington, held large tracts of land in western Pennsylvania and had sometimes evicted longtime tenants.

Although President George Washington had originally opposed the whiskey tax as unfair, he felt he had no alternative but to enforce it once Congress had enacted it. So tax collectors were appointed and distilleries were assessed.

Resistance to the tax was strong in all the Appalachian mountain states. The tax collectors were harassed. Smuggling thrived. Only a few of those taxed paid up. Nevertheless, Hamilton insisted that the law be enforced and the excise taxes be collected. An example must be set, he said, and western Pennsylvania was chosen since it was close to the federal capital at Philadelphia.

The frustrations of the frontier farmers in Pennsylvania soon led to violence. Tempers grew hot. Tax collectors were threatened, and one was even tarred and feathered. In 1792, two distillers were arrested for violating the tax law and were taken all the way to Philadelphia for trial. Seventy-five more were issued summonses.

Opposition continued to escalate. On July 15, 1794, tax collector John Neville accompanied a federal marshal who was to serve a summons on farmer William Miller. Miller refused to accept the summons, and the officials were forcibly removed from the property by a band of angry field hands. The next day, a posse of thirty farmers and sympathizers rode to Neville's home to appeal for an end to the summonses. In the confrontation, Neville and those who worked for him, including his slaves, fired on the group, killing Oliver Miller, said to be William Miller's nephew.

Outraged by this action, the western Pennsylvania farmers now mobilized 500 militiamen from four counties under Maj. James McFarlane, a Revolutionary War veteran. The troops attacked Neville's house in hopes of taking him prisoner, forcing him to resign, and capturing his

David Bradford, a well-to-do lawyer in Washington County who incited protests against the heavy tax on whiskey, lived in this house on Main Street in Washington. As the troops approached to put an end to the violence, Bradford fled to Louisiana. He never lived in the house again.

books. Both sides fired on each other. During one of several calls for a temporary truce during the gunfight, McFarlane stepped from behind the protection of a tree to shout commands to the far end of his skirmish line. A volley of gunfire rang out from the house, mortally wounding him. Angered anew by what they saw as wanton disregard of a call for a cease-fire, the militiamen burned Neville's house, Bower Hill, which had been called "the finest house in the west," to the ground, along with its barn and outbuildings, after allowing its occupants to escape.

Now a radical opponent named David Bradford, a prominent lawyer who was deputy attorney general of Washington County, stepped in. Under his leadership, a group of men robbed the mails to obtain evidence of who was in favor and who was opposed to armed insurrection. There was even talk of independence for western Pennsylvania, and a rebel flag with six stripes was created.

On August 1, Bradford and some 5,000 militiamen marched toward nearby Pittsburgh in a show of force to try to take the city, capture Fort Pitt, and gain arms and ammunition. They assembled at Braddock's

Field, the site of the earlier Battle of Monongahela in the French and Indian War (see pages 25–29), located in what is now the city of Braddock. The people of that area, wanting to avoid burning and looting, greeted the troops with conciliation, food, whiskey, and good humor. The strategy worked; the armed band quietly dispersed, and the rebels returned to their farms.

Despite this apparent cooling of the situation, President Washington on August 7 decided it was necessary to take firm action. He moved against the armed band, some of whom he had commanded during the Revolutionary War. To preserve the federal authority, he issued a proclamation requiring all insurgents to return peacefully to their homes. The federal government, he stated, "could not suffer the laws to be trampled upon with impunity for there is an end to representative government."

At the same time, he directed the raising of more than 12,000 troops from the New Jersey, Pennsylvania, Maryland, and Virginia militias to march against the defiant farmers. Ironically, it was the largest number of troops Washington had ever directed, even more than his commands during the Revolution.

Realizing they were in jeopardy, on August 14 farmers from six western Pennsylvania counties held another mass meeting at Parkinson's Ferry on the Monongahela River to respond to Washington's decree. After heated discussions, the participants agreed to moderate the strategy that had thus far been pursued by the radical insurrectionists among them. They appointed a committee of sixty, which in turn elected two members to meet with Washington and Secretary of the Treasury Alexander Hamilton, who by now were on their way from Philadelphia in advance of the army.

Another meeting was held on August 23 at Parkinson's Ferry to elect a committee of twelve, with Albert Gallatin as its leader. The committee's purpose was to hold a conference with a state peacemaking delegation at Redstone Old Fort to appease the approaching army, but the committee was unable to arrange the conference.

Later that fall, the federal troops reached Somerset County. President Washington, quartered in the Espy House in Bedford, was determined to end the insurrection, using force if necessary. In a last-ditch attempt to forestall the army's march, two delegates from the insurgents met with President Washington on October 9 but were unable to persuade him to stop the march.

Not until October 24 did the troops enter the Monongahela Valley. During the week of November 5 to 13, they marched to Parkinson's Ferry and the Mingo settlement in Washington County to make arrests.

They met no resistance. The soldiers took a number of farmers as pris-oners. They were treated brutally by the troops, who held them in cellars and open stockades during the cold weather, causing the freez-ing night of November 13 to be forever remembered as "That Terrible Night."

David Bradford, the incendiary leader of the insurrection, escaped the advancing army on a coal barge down the Monongahela and Ohio Rivers. After reaching Louisiana, then Spanish territory, he became a wealthy plantation owner and built an ornate Southern home. Several years later, he sent for his family and sold his home in Washington.

On November 16, the federal troops left the valley to return to Philadelphia with their prisoners—a few hapless farmers, many of whom had never actually lifted a hand or a weapon against the government. Their trials were held a full five months later in May 1795. As a result, both the guilty and the innocent were pardoned, but only after all had signed an act of submission to the federal government.

The Whiskey Tax was later modified by Congress to make it more agreeable and affordable to the taxed farmers. It was repealed entirely after Thomas Jefferson became president. The quelling of the Whiskey Rebellion confirmed the power of the central government to control anarchy in the country. But it also demonstrated to those in the affluent East how vulnerable the western settlers were. As a result, it brought increased help to the frontiersmen in protecting them against maraud-ing Indians.

WHAT YOU SEE TODAY

David Bradford House. The home built in 1788 by David Brad-ford is an elegant one for what was then a frontier town. Its handsome stairway is solid mahogany. Mantelpieces and other interior furnishings were carried over the Allegheny Mountains from Philadelphia at great expense. Other woodwork in the home was imported from England. Located at 175 Main Street in Washington, Pennsylvania, 25 miles southwest of Pittsburgh, the home has been restored by the Pennsyl-vania Historical and Museum Commission.

When to visit: May to December, Wednesday to Saturday, 11 A.M. to 4 P.M.; Sunday by appointment.

Admission fees: Adults $4, seniors $3.50, students $2.

Special events: October: reenactment of Bradford's escape; first week-end of December: candlelight tour.

Tours of the site: Daily, when house is open.

Time needed to visit: One hour.

Special considerations: First floor is handicapped accessible.
Parking: Free, in rear.
Gift shop: Books, pamphlets, and memorabilia.
Directions: The David Bradford House is three blocks from the Washington County courthouse on Main Street in the town of Washington.

Other Whiskey Rebellion sites

Neville House. Residence built in 1785 by Revolutionary War general John Neville, the chief tax collector in western Pennsylvania at the time of the Whiskey Rebellion. When his home, Bower Hill, was burned, he fled to Woodville, a home his son then lived in. Now a museum, it is located in Bridgeville, Allegheny County. Call 412-471-5808 to arrange a house tour.

Oliver Miller Homestead. Open to visitors who want to see a typical home of the period. The owner of the original log house, Oliver Miller, was killed when the insurgents attacked Bower Hill, the nearby home of John Neville on July 14, 1794. The reconstructed 1808 stone house is preserved within a 2,000-acre Allegheny County recreation area called South Park. It is located in Library, Pennsylvania, off PA Route 88 at the corner of Corrigan Drive and Stone Manse Drive. Open Sunday, 1 P.M. to 4 P.M.

David Espy House. Located at 123 Pitt Street, Bradford, this National Historic Landmark was built in 1766. It served as headquarters for President George Washington when he led federal troops to western Pennsylvania in 1794 to quell the Whiskey Rebellion. A bakery now occupies the site.

Friendship Hill National Historic Site. Preserves the country estate of Albert Gallatin, a Swiss immigrant who served as secretary of the treasury under the presidents Thomas Jefferson and James Madison. Friendship Hill features an exhibit room with information and a presentation about Gallatin's life. Among his many accomplishments as financier, diplomat, entrepeneur, and politician was the financing of the Louisiana Purchase and the Lewis and Clark Expedition. Gallatin played an important role as a peacemaker in the Whiskey Rebellion. Twelve miles south of Uniontown, near Point Marion on the banks of the Monongahela River, Friendship Hill is open daily year-round except Christmas Day.

Mingo Meetinghouse and Cemetery. A monument commemorates the location of the original Presbyterian meetinghouse where the "Mingo Creek boys" met to plan an armed insurrection against the new federal government. A modern church now stands on the site. A tomb-

President George Washington stayed at the Espy House on Pitt Street in Bedford when he led troops to western Pennsylvania in 1791 to quell the Whiskey Rebellion. The event remains the only time in U.S. history that a sitting president actively led an armed force.

stone that marks the grave of Maj. James McFarlane, who led the attack by the local militia on the tax collector's home, states that the officer was "slain by an unprincipled villain."

Tourist information

Washington County Tourism Promotion Agency, Washington Crown Center, 1500 West Chestnut Street, Washington, PA 15301, telephone 800-531-4114, website www.washpatourism.org.

Other nearby sites

LeMoyne House and Gardens. The 1812 stone mansion, office, and apothecary of Dr. Francis LeMoyne, an antislavery advocate, is now the home of the Washington County Historical Society. The LeMoyne House served as a station on the Underground Railroad. The house is open February to December, Tuesday through Friday, 11 A.M. to 4 P.M.; and Saturday and Sunday, 12 noon to 4 P.M. For more information, call 724-225-6740.

Erie Maritime Museum and US Brig *Niagara*

BATTLE OF LAKE ERIE, WAR OF 1812

150 East Front Street
Erie, PA 16503
814-452-2744
website: www.brigniagara.org

Scarcely three decades after the American Revolution, the newly created United States found itself caught up in a general European conflict, one that the new nation had tried hard to avoid. Europe's two most powerful nations, France and Great Britain, had battled almost continuously since 1793. Now Britain was trying to defeat Napoleon I, who had conquered other European countries, forcing them into his French Empire.

This warfare between the two major European powers directly affected American trade. No less than 1,500 American vessels had been seized between 1803 and 1812. The Americans grew increasingly angry over British attacks on their ships, which prevented American cargoes from reaching France and were bringing the growing American economy almost to the point of collapse.

The Americans had a second quarrel with Britain, a country that had dominated the seas since the British Navy defeated the French in the Battle of Trafalgar in 1805. British ship captains often stopped neutral U.S. ships on the high seas, boarded the vessels, and seized seamen, a tactic called impressment. Each British sailor bore a tattoo on his wrist, proof to the authorities that he was an English seaman. When a British officer boarded an American ship, he ordered all the sailors to "present arms" so he could identify tattoos and reclaim any British deserters. The Americans claimed that the British were seizing not only British sailors who had illegally deserted from the British Navy, but also a sizable number of U.S. citizens—estimates suggest 6,000 or more.

But perhaps the most basic disagreement that led the U.S. to declare war on Great Britain in the War of 1812 had nothing to do with rights on the high seas, but with territory in North America and the U.S. desire to push the British out of the Great Lakes region, thereby preventing them from forming alliances with the American Indians.

125

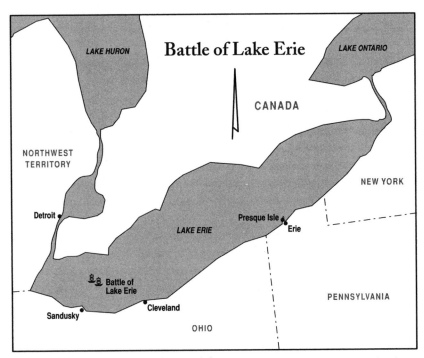

This major sea battle in the heart of the new nation was a turning point in the War of 1812 and helped persuade Great Britain to negotiate an end to the conflict, confirming that the Northwest Territory was part of the United States.

Some radicals in the United States even hoped to evict the British from all of Canada, thus gaining control of all of northern North America.

During the first two years of the war, however, the U.S. land forces were no match for the well-trained British Army, surrendering Detroit and losing several other battles. The warfare even spread to the South, where Maj. Gen. Andrew Jackson defeated the Creek Indians, who were allies of the British. Other U.S. Navy warships, such as the *Constitution*, or "Old Ironsides," won victories in the Atlantic.

It became clear early in the war that Lake Erie was vital to the control of what was then called the Northwest Territory, the lands that lay south of the Great Lakes. In order for the U.S. Army to advance into Canada, it was essential to move troops and supplies across Lake Erie. But at the war's beginning, Britain—possessor of the mightiest navy in the world—controlled the Great Lakes from its Canadian bases with its fleet of sailing ships.

So the Americans decided to counter the British with a Great Lakes fleet of their own. A twenty-seven-year-old naval officer, Oliver Hazard Perry, was selected to expedite the construction of the ships and then take command of the new U.S. squadron. Within nine months, after overcoming many obstacles, two armed brigs and four schooners were completed at Erie and launched into adjacent Presque Isle Bay. Three smaller vessels were brought from the eastern end of the lake, slipping past the British and joining the newly constructed ships in the bay. The mouth of the bay, enclosed within the fishhook-shaped peninsula of Presque Isle, was guarded by a protective sandbar. The strategic sandbar, an underwater ridge, protected the ships within the bay while preventing the British ships from entering. The British sailing offshore kept a close watch on this activity, knowing they would soon face this new fleet. But because of the sandbar, they were unable to reach their quarry.

In August 1813, the British ships mysteriously disappeared, possibly to reprovision. Now the Americans, using a clever engineering feat developed in the Netherlands, floated their newly built warships over the shallow sandbar and out onto Lake Erie to be ready for battle. The two heavier ships, *Lawrence* and *Niagara*, were stripped of their guns and heavy equipment to make them as light as possible. The *Lawrence* went first. Two large barges, or floats, called "camels," were placed on either side of the ship and filled with water. Beams were fixed to the camels and attached to the ship through the sweep (oar) ports. Then the water was pumped out and the camels rose, buoying up the ship's keel so the vessel could be successfully eased over the shallow sandbar and out onto the lake. Once the brig was floating free, its guns and equipment were reinstalled.

As the second ship, the *Niagara*, was being eased over the sandbar, the British fleet suddenly reappeared. But the British commander, Lt. Robert H. Barclay, declined to fight, deciding he would wait until his newly built ship, the *Detroit*, could be added to his fleet.

Soon the American fleet of nine vessels was ready to do battle. At daybreak on September 10, 1813, Perry's lookout sighted the British fleet of six vessels at the western end of Lake Erie. At this point, the two fleets were fairly evenly matched; however, the British had more long-range cannons, while the Americans had more short-range guns, called carronades.

The sea battle began at 11:45 A.M. as the British took advantage of their long-range cannons. Barclay's flagship, the newly built *Detroit*,

The battling Brig Niagara *sails again! Victor over the British squadron in the War of 1812, the restored* Niagara *is once again fully operational and takes part with other tall ships in nautical commemorative events. When at her home port, the ship ties up at the Erie Maritime Museum.*

pounded Perry's flagship, the *Lawrence*. Perry, with a light wind at his back, could only sail slowly into the teeth of this bombardment until his ship's carronades were within range. Although the *Lawrence* was suffering severe damage, the *Niagara* inexplicably hung back, not attacking the *Queen Charlotte* as planned, but staying out of the battle.

The now unchallenged *Queen Charlotte* also pounded the *Lawrence*. On the Lawrence, Kentucky riflemen in the rigging sniped at the British, taking a cruel toll as the brigs hammered at each other. Perry strode the deck, directing his ship's cannon fire, miraculously unhurt while others died around him. Every officer except Perry and his midshipman younger brother, Alexander, who had been knocked unconscious, was either dead or wounded. The brig's sailing master described "a picture too horrid for description—nearly the whole crew and officers all prostrated on the deck, intermingled with broken spars, riggings, sails." By 2:30 P.M., four of every five men on the ship were killed or wounded, and all of her guns were out of action.

Perry then made a desperate decision. Knowing that the *Lawrence* was all but disabled, he took command of one of the *Lawrence's* small boats (amazingly, one was still seaworthy), and with cannonballs and small arms fire hissing overhead transferred to the undamaged *Niagara*. Taking charge, he daringly directed the *Niagara* straight toward the British ships, some of which were in trouble themselves. Both the *Detroit* and the *Queen Charlotte* had been badly damaged by the American carronades. Captain Barclay was wounded, and every other British commander was either killed or wounded.

When they saw the *Niagara* coming, the British tried to maneuver the *Detroit* and the *Queen Charlotte* into better firing position, but instead they rammed each other, their sails and spars tangling irretrievably. Perry sailed the *Niagara* right through the middle of the British line, raking the ships on both sides with his heavy guns. The battle lasted only fifteen more minutes, until the British struck their colors and surrendered.

It was an important but costly victory. The *Lawrence* had borne the worst of the fighting; twenty-two of the twenty-seven American men killed in the battle were from her decks, as were two-thirds of the ninety-six wounded. On the British side, forty-one men were killed and ninety-two wounded. Perry was the first in U.S. history to defeat an entire British squadron and successfully bring back every enemy ship to his base as a prize of war. Soon after the battle, he penned his famous note to Maj. Gen. William Henry Harrison: "We have met the enemy and they are ours: two ships, two brigs, one schooner and one sloop."

Lake Erie was now in American hands, and by September 27, Perry's fleet had ferried Major General Harrison's army across Lake Erie to the Canadian mainland. The British Army abandoned Fort Malden near Detroit and retreated up the Thames River in Canada. Harrison's forces followed and decisively defeated the British forces in a sharp battle. The great Indian leader Tecumseh, who led the Indian allies of the British, was killed in that battle. With him died the Indian and British hopes for domination of the Northwest Territory. By defeating the British on both sea and land, the Americans took control of Lake Erie and with it most of the Northwest Territory. The Battle of Lake Erie was a turning point and helped persuade the British to negotiate an end to the war. At the peace talks that ended the War of 1812 a year later at Ghent, Belgium, the United States claimed sovereignty over the Northwest Territory. Both parties at the peace talks sensed that the United States had emerged from the conflict full of confidence, with a stronger sense of nationhood, and had rid itself of the last vestiges of dependence upon Europe.

The Great Lakes battle was one of the few American successes in a war that was far from popular and of which both sides had wearied. The end of the fighting produced no clear winner, but for the United States, the Northwest Territory was now secure and its boundaries undisputed, giving Americans room to expand. Among the real winners in the War of 1812 were those Americans who dreamed of settling in the Great Lakes region. The way was now cleared for them. The biggest losers, as usual, were the Indians, who had sided with the British. They were pushed out of their traditional homeland, losing both their homes and their hunting grounds as the American settlers moved ever westward.

WHAT YOU SEE TODAY

Erie Maritime Museum. Serves as home port for the reconstructed US Brig *Niagara*, which lies berthed within view from a bayside window at the museum. Erie is Pennsylvania's only port on Lake Erie and is the state's gateway to the Great Lakes. Inside, the museum exhibits and films illustrate the War of 1812 and the Battle of Lake Erie. A replica of the midship section of the US Brig *Lawrence*, which has been fired upon, discloses the damaging effects of actual cannonballs and shot. Visitors also view a foretop section of a square-rigged sailing ship. Other areas of the innovative museum relate the environmental history of the Great Lakes and tell of the USS *Michigan* (later *Wolverine*), the U.S. Navy's first iron warship, which was built and stationed in the Great Lakes for seventy-five years.

US Brig Niagara. A reconstruction of Perry's ship (1 percent of the ship is original). The vessel is fully operational, with a crew of fifteen professional sailors and twenty-five volunteers for each voyage. Volunteers from across the country may sign on for a period of weeks or months. The brig is on exhibit most days at the museum in odd-numbered years; in even-numbered years, she fulfills a schedule of sailing events on the East Coast or Great Lakes region. When in Erie, the *Niagara* conducts short sorties into Lake Erie to train crew members. Occasionally, the ship takes part with other tall ships of the world in major commemorative events of international interest.

When to visit: Open Monday through Saturday, 9 A.M. to 5 P.M.; Sunday 12 noon to 5 P.M.

Admission fees: Museum and Brig *Niagara* adults $6, seniors $5, children $3.

Special events: June: Erie Festival of the Arts, living-history weekend with an encampment and demonstrations by reenactors. Also, other living-history appearances, gallery talks, and special demonstrations.

Tours of the site: Regular tours by staff and volunteers.

Time needed to visit: Two hours.

Special considerations: Museum is handicapped accessible; touring the brig requires climbing stairs and stooping low. Since the Brig *Niagara* has an active sailing schedule, call ahead to make sure the ship will be in port.

Parking: Free on-site parking.

Gift shop: Memorabilia, souvenirs, clothing, books, and reproduction prints.

Directions: On the waterfront in downtown Erie, at Bayfront Highway and Holland Street.

Tourist information

Erie Area Convention and Visitors Bureau, 1006 State Street, Erie, PA 16507, telephone 814-454-7191, fax 814-459-0241, website www.eriepa.com, e-mail erie-tourism@erie.net.

Other nearby sites

Presque Isle State Park. Presque Isle means "almost an island." A tour road circles the peninsula along the shore of Presque Isle Bay, which includes Misery Bay, where six of Perry's ships anchored until they could pass over the sandbar at its entrance. After the battle, Perry and his men returned to Misery Bay to repair their ships and treat the wounded, many of whom later suffered from smallpox. Those who died during the winter of 1813–14 were buried under the ice in nearby Grave Yard Pond. A monument at Crystal Point at the tip of Misery Bay commemorates the American victory in the Battle of Lake Erie. The 74-foot-high Presque Isle Lighthouse, the second built on Lake Erie, still guides ships on the lake. The day-use park, designated as a National Natural Landmark, has 13 miles of hiking trails, swimming beaches, boating, fishing, water skiing, and picnic pavilions.

Site of Fort Presque Isle. A historical marker at Sixth Street and Parade Street designates the site of the fort, built by the French in 1753 and abandoned in 1759. The British, under Col. Henry Bouquet, built a second fort in 1760, which was captured by the Indians in 1763 during Pontiac's Rebellion (see page 104). At Sixth Street and Ash Street is another historical marker at the restored blockhouse of the later American Fort Presque Isle. This was the original burial site of Gen. Anthony Wayne who died there on December 15, 1796.

Erie History Center at Discovery Square. The center, in an 1840s building at 417 State Street, includes changing exhibits on local industry and architecture, a library, and archives. The 1839 Cashier's House and the residence of the chief officer of the United States Bank are located next door. Walking and driving tours are available. The center is open Tuesday through Saturday, 9 A.M. to 5 P.M.; the Cashier's House is open Tuesday through Saturday, 1 P.M. to 4 P.M. For more information, call 814-454-1813.

LANDMARKS
OF THE
CIVIL WAR

Hanover Landmarks

Hanover Area Historical Society
Box 305
105 High Street
Hanover, PA 17331
717-632-3207
fax: 717-632-5199
e-mail: carbrn@blazenet.net

It was June 1863. After much fighting in Virginia, including the hard-fought Confederate victory at Chancellorsville scarcely a month before, Gen. Robert E. Lee and the Confederate leaders were determined to take the war to the North.

Lee's army moved northward, following the natural pathway offered by the Shenandoah Valley. The Union Army, numbering some 65,000 men and now under the command of Gen. George G. Meade, moved northward as well, staying well to the east of the Confederates to protect the cities of Washington and Baltimore, both important supply points for the Federals.

Meanwhile, a Confederate cavalry brigade of 5,000 men under Maj. Gen. J. E. B. Stuart made a dramatic—and risky—swing to the east around the advancing Union Army. At Rockville, Maryland, a scant 15 miles west of Washington, the daring Southerners captured a long wagon train loaded with oats, whiskey, bacon, hams, and sugar. In taking this action, Stuart was carrying out Lee's orders to collect all the supplies he could for the use of the army. Damaged wagons, along with supplies that could not be carried, were burned.

But Stuart now found himself with a slow-moving wagon train to pull along, as well as more than 100 prisoners to guard. Furthermore, in his zeal to acquire supplies, his cavalry force had become disconnected from the main Confederate invading force that was headed in the direction of Harrisburg. Lee hoped to attack or capture the Pennsylvania capital and destroy its railroad yards and rolling stock. The loss of Pennsylvania's state capital would have been a significant blow to Northern morale. Without Stuart's cavalry, however, Lee found himself deprived of his "eyes and ears" during this fateful march into the North, an offensive that culminated in the Battle of Gettysburg.

That was the picture on June 30 when Stuart, his cavalry, and his rumbling wagon train made their way toward the town of Hanover,

10 miles north of the Maryland border. Hanover, a small agricultural town, was similar to Gettysburg in that it was at the juncture of several roads, which made it a trading hub. Its residents kept cows, horses, pigs, and chickens in backyard stables and coops. At the time of the battle, the town had nineteen wagon-making shops, seventeen black-smith shops, and twelve cigar factories. As a crossroads for teamsters and Conestoga wagons, it also had a number of taverns with yards to accommodate horses and wagons. Railroads had been constructed within the past ten years to connect it with nearby towns.

To their surprise, the Confederates discovered that a Union cavalry force of 4,000 men under Maj. Gen. Judson Kilpatrick was just then marching through Hanover and on out the Abbotstown Road (now Broadway), the troops forming a column 8 miles long. Only a short while before, the townspeople had been out in the streets of town welcoming the Union horsemen, offering food and water as the soldiers moved through. Now the rear guard of the Union column—the 18th Pennsylvania Regiment, led by Lt. Col. William P. Brinton—was approaching town.

Without warning, a force of Confederate cavalrymen attacked this unit at the rear of the column. A wild chase ensued, as the Pennsylva-nians galloped toward town. Fighting soon raged through the streets. Horsemen became mixed with runaway wagons, ambulances, and pan-icked citizens. Soldiers and civilians alike ran into alleys and down side streets. An officer of the 5th New York Regiment was shot in the eye, the ball passing completely through his head, killing him instantly. Soon the Confederate forces gained control of the town.

As soon as they heard the sounds of gunfire back in town, the Union commanders at the head of the long Union column turned several of their units around and sent them speedily back to do battle. With Kilpatrick himself in the lead, the Federals drove back the South-erners out of town and regained control. They then barricaded the streets with store boxes, hay ladders, fence rails, and bar iron to pre-vent the Confederates from retaking the town.

During the confusion, Stuart himself narrowly evaded capture. Trying to get close to the action, he discovered that he and an aide were directly in front of a charging blue cavalry line. Finding them-selves potentially trapped, they jumped their horses over a 15-foot gully and escaped back to their own lines. A drainage ditch still remains today in a suburban neighborhood, a reminder of this obstacle that Stuart overcame.

Artillery now kept both sides apart. Confederate cannons placed in an elevated field south of town (now the site of a golf course) dueled with Union artillery on the north side. Shells burst into Hanover's streets, pinning down some of the Federals and damaging buildings. No civilians were injured, although a number of Union troopers were.

At one house in town, the Winebrenner House, a mother and her daughter took the risk of stepping out on the rear balcony of their home. They saw a flash of a cannon shot from a hill perhaps 800 yards away and had barely stepped back into the room when a cannonball smashed through the lintel behind them, fortunately missing both.

As the afternoon wore on, Stuart became concerned because he knew that more Union troops were in the vicinity and might arrive on the battlefield at any time. He was also aware that his orders called for his cavalry to rendezvous with other Confederate forces at York, which lay 20 miles to the northeast, and he wanted to protect his wagon train with its much-needed supplies. Since he was out of contact with Lee's main army, however, he did not realize that Lee had ordered all Confederate forces to gather at Cashtown near Gettysburg, 20 miles to the west, in anticipation of a major battle with the Union forces. So at nightfall, Stuart ordered his troops to withdraw and resume their march eastward toward York. To free himself for action, he later released his prisoners and sent the captured wagon train southward. The Battle of Hanover was ended.

Kilpatrick knew from scouting reports that a large part of the main Confederate Army was nearby and thus did not pursue Stuart eastward. Instead, he took his force straight to Gettysburg and participated in the battle, while Stuart's cavalry was lost to Lee and the Confederates until the last day of the Battle of Gettysburg.

Casualty figures for the engagement list Union losses at more than 200, including 19 killed. Incomplete casualty figures for the Confederates cite 55 killed or wounded.

The significance of the Battle of Hanover is that it diverted Stuart's cavalry, preventing it from joining other Confederate forces that were soon involved in the critical battle at Gettysburg. Stuart, out of touch with the main Confederate Army, learned too late of Lee's plans for the major engagement at Gettysburg, and thus the Southern cavalry played only a minor role on the last day of the battle. Furthermore, Lee, left without the intelligence he expected from Stuart, was unable to properly assess the size and disposition of the Union forces that opposed him at Gettysburg.

Eleven Union soldiers who fought in the Battle of Hanover lie buried under this row of tombstones beside the war monument and a Civil War cannon at Mount Olivet Cemetery.

WHAT YOU SEE TODAY

Hanover Square. Typical of many Pennsylvania town squares, Hanover Square looks much the way it did during the 1863 battle. The old Central Hotel, where Kilpatrick made his headquarters, still stands on the square; it now is called the Central Building and contains retail stores and apartments. Built in 1810, it originally served as an inn and stage office on the road between Frederick, Maryland, and York, Pennsylvania. At one side of the square stand two Union Parrott rifle cannons. These two pieces were among the first ones of their type to be manufactured during the war. Nearby is a plaque marking the site where one of the Union commanders, Brig. Gen. George Armstrong Custer, tied his horse to a tree. Custer later gained notoriety as the U.S. Army cavalry officer who lost his life in Montana at the Battle of Little Bighorn against an Indian contingent in 1876. Across the square, a mounted statue represents all the Union cavalrymen who fought at Hanover. Called *The Picket*, the horseman appears to be watching for signs of the enemy and represents scouts that were sent out as lookouts to spot opposing forces.

Winebrenner House. A Federal-style residence at 234 Frederick Street, built in 1792 by a prosperous leather tanner. During the battle, Confederate cannonballs pierced a balcony door, smashed through a chest of drawers inside, and came to rest in the basement. The mother and daughter barely escaped injury while the rest of the family sought safety in the cellar. The hole remains in the original door. Two cannonballs that crashed through the door are on display at the Hanover Area Historical Society. In addition to the Winebrenner House, a number of other historic homes in Hanover display bronze plaques identifying them as houses that stood at the time of the engagement. Near the Samuel Keller farmhouse, which dates back to the time of the battle, archaeologists have recovered bullets fired by Spencer rifles. The 7-shot Spencer repeating rifles were used only by some Union soldiers.

Mount Olivet Cemetery. This cemetery at 725 Baltimore Street, located on a low hill near where Confederate artillery was emplaced during the battle, it is the burial site for a number of Union soldiers who fought in the Battle of Hanover. A monument of a soldier, flanked by two cannons, commemorates the war dead. Its inscription reads:

> On fame's eternal camping-ground
> Their silent tents are spread
> And Glory guards with solemn round
> The bivouac of the dead.

Neas House. A brick home at 113 West Chestnut Street built in 1783 by Mathias Neas, a successful tanner. The home combines the typical architectural styles then common in cities like Philadelphia. Original rafters and beams can be seen in the cellar and kitchen. It has nine fireplaces in all. Restored through local funding, the Neas House, along with a nearby building, serves as the headquarters for the Hanover Area Historical Society. Open May through October, Tuesday through Friday, 10 A.M. to 1 P.M.

Lincoln Plaque. On Carlisle Street near the railway station, the plaque commemorates the spot where Pres. Abraham Lincoln on November 18, 1863, came out on the rear platform of his railroad car, while his locomotive stopped to take on water, to speak to the townspeople on his way to deliver his Gettysburg Address. According to accounts of the time, after the crowd at the depot called loudly for him to speak, he said, "Well, you have seen me, and according to general experience you have seen less than you expected to see." Then he added a cautionary comment about the earlier Battle of Hanover: "I trust that when the enemy was here the citizens of Hanover were loyal to our country and the Stars and Stripes. If you are not all true patriots in support of the Union you should be."

Mason-Dixon Line Marker. Just off U.S. Route 94, south of Hanover, this is one of the few remaining stones marking what became the dividing line between the North and South during the Civil War. The limestone marker was one of those brought from England as ballast in a sailing ship and set out at each mile by surveyors Charles Mason and Jeremiah Dixon. The line was ordered to be surveyed by proprietors Thomas and Richard Penn, sons of William Penn, to establish a permanent border between Maryland, Delaware, and Pennsylvania and to help settle land disputes. Mason and Dixon completed their survey in 1767.

Hanover Public Library. The library's Pennsylvania Room, on the second floor, contains old maps of the region, family Bibles, old manuscripts, newspaper clippings, microfilmed local newspapers dating back to 1800, and genealogical references. Located on Library Place. For more information, call 717-632-5183.

Hanover Area Historical Society. Preserves artifacts, deeds, indentures, photographs, genealogical records, family Bibles, and early tax records. Open Monday, Wednesday, and Friday, 9 A.M. to 1 P.M.

When to visit: Each season has its special charm, but spring and summer offer more visitor opportunities.

Admission fees: Free.

Special events: July: Dutch Days, a community-wide event with craft displays and sales, fun foods, tours of historic homes, classic automobiles, music, and entertainment; third Sunday in August: ice cream social at Wirt Park.

Tours of the site: Hanover Area Historical Society provides booklets for self-guided historic walking tours and road tours.

Time needed to visit: Plan on one full day to explore the historic sites and local scenery.

Special considerations: Most of Hanover attractions are handicapped accessible, but it would be advisable to check for special considerations.

Parking: On-street.

Gift shop: Books and historical materials.

Directions: Take U.S. Route 30 west from York or east to Gettysburg, then follow PA Route 116 (Hanover Road) to Hanover.

Tourist information

Hanover Area Chamber of Commerce, 146 Carlisle Street, Hanover, PA 17331, telephone at 717-637-6130.

Other nearby sites

Hanover Fire Museum and Hanover Fire Station #1. Houses an 1881 Silsby steam fire engine, as well as early fire memorabilia. Located at 201 North Franklin Street. For more information, call 717-630-2390.

York. The nation's capital from September 30, 1777 to June 27, 1778. The late eighteenth century is preserved in the restored Golden Plough Tavern, General Horatio Gates House, and the Bobb Log House. Located at 157 West Market Street. A block away is the York County Colonial Court House, where the Continental Congress voted to adopt the Articles of Confederation. The York County Heritage Trust is nearby, at 250 East Market Street, with exhibits of early York County life. For information, call 717-848-1587.

Chambersburg Landmarks

Kittochtinny Historical Society
175 East King Street
Chambersburg, PA 17201
717-264-1667
website: www.chambersburg.org

The town of Chambersburg, situated in the broad Cumberland Valley, 15 miles north of the Maryland border, lay in the natural pathway northward for Lee's invading army during the Civil War. It is hardly surprising, then, that Chambersburg was subjected to three Confederate raids in three years of war.

Chambersburg at the time was a small farming community. In the surrounding Pennsylvania farmland, especially among the Pennsylvania Dutch, who were German settlers with a strong tradition of ethnic separation, there was little interest in or sympathy for the war. "The country people displayed entire indifference," one correspondent wrote. "They say the war is a mere quarrel between abolitionists and secessionists and that they did not care which won. . . . They would be glad to have peace on any terms."

The first incursion by the Confederates into the lives of these townspeople was in October 1862. After their hard-won victory at Antietam, 40 miles to the south of Chambersburg, the Confederates seized the initiative in the war. Under orders from Lee to harass the Union forces and to obtain much-needed food and supplies, Gen. J. E. B. Stuart and an 1,800-man cavalry force left the Potomac River behind, crossed the Mason-Dixon Line for the first time, and moved into the North, occupying Chambersburg with little opposition.

"Our people were confounded with astonishment at the brilliant audacity of the rebels penetrating 20 miles in [the Union] rear," wrote A. K. McClure, editor of the Chambersburg newspaper, who witnessed the event. The few home guards on duty in the town, he said, were no match for the Confederates' mounted cavalry and artillery.

Capturing the town, the Southerners took some 800 horses and seized stocks of shoes, clothing, and ammunition. Many of these supplies had been captured by the Union forces from the Confederates in prior actions. What the invaders could not take with them they destroyed by burning—the railroad station house, the roundhouse, machine shops, and warehouses filled with ammunition.

After one night of occupation, McClure wrote, the invaders left town "thanking me for the hospitality they had received. We parted, mutually expressing the hope that should we meet again it would be under more pleasant circumstances." After raiding Chambersburg, the Confederates then rode south again, crossed back over the Potomac, and rejoined Lee's army in Virginia with their newly acquired supplies to replenish the Confederate troops.

Eight months later, in late June 1863, the Confederates swept through Chambersburg once more as Lee's army invaded the North in an offensive aimed at capturing Harrisburg, a drive that culminated in the decisive Battle of Gettysburg. Lee hoped that this invasion would encourage the North to negotiate a peace treaty with the South and persuade England and France to support the Southern cause. As before, the Confederate troops seized any horses they could find and helped themselves to chickens, pigs, geese, beef, and flour from the farms in the area, paying for some with Confederate money and expropriating others. Some 70,000 Confederate troops camped for one night east of the town.

The most devastating attack on Chambersburg, however, occurred a year later, on a hot day in July 1864, when the Confederates held the town ransom in retribution for the burning of Southern homes by Union forces. The local militiamen who might have protected the town had been pulled away to bolster the Union Army of the Potomac, leaving Chambersburg virtually defenseless. A Confederate cavalry force of 3,000 under the command of Gen. John McCausland, acting under orders from Gen. Jubal Early, formed up west of town. Its artillery sent several warning shells into the unprotected town.

Finding no opposition, McCausland rode into town with some 800 men. After insolently helping himself to breakfast at a local hotel, he ordered the courthouse bell to be rung to summon residents to the town square. When no one appeared, he rounded up six prominent citizens and presented them with an order from Gen. Jubal Early: the citizens were to raise $100,000 in gold or $500,000 in Northern currency as ransom. If the town failed to comply, it would be burned. The citizens could not have complied with the order even if they wanted to, however, since many had sent their money to banks in Philadelphia for safekeeping because of their proximity to the South and their vulnerability to invasion. Therefore, the ransom could not be raised.

So McCausland gave the order and soldiers battered down doors and entered houses, broke up furniture for kindling, doused it with kerosene, and set the houses afire. Some soldiers stole silverware, jewelry, and liquor. "Many families escaped with only the clothing they had on," wrote an eyewitness. "In many cases they were not allowed to take these, but were threatened with instant death if they did not cast them away and flee. Sick and aged people had to be carried to the fields."

"As to the result," this inhabitant concluded, "I may say that the entire heart or body of the town is burned. Not a house or building of any kind is left on a space of about, on average, two squares of streets, extending each way from the centre, with some four or five exceptions, where the buildings were isolated. Only the outskirts are left."

More than 300 dwellings, shops, and buildings in the center of town were destroyed. Women, children, and the elderly were forced into the street. Three thousand were left homeless as the town was left a smoldering ruin, the only Northern town burned by regular Confederate forces during the war.

WHAT YOU SEE TODAY

Old Jail. A well-restored brick structure at the corner of Second Street and King Street, the Old Jail survived the fire of 1864 and is the third-oldest building in Chambersburg. In its cellar are five domed dungeons with rings in the walls and floors that were used to tie down prisoners. These cells were also used, historians say, as safe hiding places for runaway slaves when it was a station on the Underground Railroad. A gallows still stands in its courtyard. The building also contains a museum of local artifacts, including period clothing, antique dishes, Indian weapons and utensils, a pioneer kitchen, an early drugstore, antique toys, and a gun collection. The second floor is occupied by the Kittochtinny Historical Society and contains a library of books and manuscripts on history and local genealogy that provides professional assistance for researchers. Free tours of the Old Jail and museum are offered during scheduled hours. Local guides add interesting stories about the area and its history. Open in summer, Tuesday, 5 to 8 P.M.; Wednesday through Saturday, 9:30 A.M. to 4 P.M.

Memorial Square. Typical of early town plans in Pennsylvania, the square, locally known as the Diamond, is the focal point of town. Today U.S. Route 11 and U.S. Route 30 intersect at the square. It was also at a crossroads on June 26, 1863, when Gen. Robert E. Lee met in the square with Gen. A. P. Hill. As a result of this conference, they agreed to move their troops eastward to Gettysburg, 25 miles away, toward what Lee believed would be an imminent battle with the Union Army. A Pennsylvania historical marker at the square describes

A determined Union soldier faces south toward the Confederacy at a memorial fountain in the town square of Chambersburg.

the meeting. A memorial fountain, dedicated in 1878, stands in the center of the square. A statue of a Union soldier faces south, as if protecting the town against a return of Confederate troops. A large granite marker, which was installed in 1893 and has a time capsule embedded in its base, commemorates the burning of Chambersburg in 1864.

Chambers Fort. A reconstruction of the log house built by Col. Benjamin Chambers in 1756 at the confluence of Falling Spring and Conococheague Creeks. Chambers operated a water-powered sawmill and gristmill. A stockade surrounded the compound to protect it from possible Indian attack. In June 1755, a Revolutionary War company called the Chambers Rifles was recruited from the area under the leadership of Capt. James Chambers, son of Benjamin Chambers, the town's founder. From this fort, the company marched 450 miles to take part in the siege of Boston.

Franklin County Courthouse. This building was the headquarters of the provost marshal of Ewell's Corps in 1864. Here General McCausland issued the ransom ultimatum. The building was gutted in the fire but later renovated.

When to visit: Although each season has its special appeal, spring and summer offer more visitor opportunities.

Admission fees: None.

Special events: July: Old Market Day includes a Civil War encampment and skirmish, historic house tours, and ChambersFest Civil War Seminar, which has prominent historians, professors, and authors presenting seminars on aspects of the Civil War. Other events include battlefield tours, book signings, receptions, and exhibits. Register through the Chambersburg Chamber of Commerce, 717-264-7101.

Tours of the site: The Cumberland Valley Visitor Station offers visitor brochures and booklets for self-guided tours of Chambersburg.

Time needed to visit: Plan on one full day to explore the historic sites and interesting local scenery.

Special considerations: Most of Chambersburg is handicapped accessible, but it is advisable to check first.

Parking: On-street.

Gift shop: The Cumberland Valley Visitor Station offers historical information and souvenirs.

Directions: From I-81, take U.S. Route 30 1 mile east.

Tourist information

Cumberland Valley Visitor Station, 1235 Lincoln Highway East, Chambersburg, PA 17201, telephone 717-261-1200 or 717-249-4801, website www.parainbow.com.

Other nearby sites

John Brown House. The abolitionist stayed here while he planned his 1859 raid on Harpers Ferry. This house was also a stop on the Underground Railroad that assisted slaves trying to escape from their owners in the South. Located at 225 East King Street.

Fort Frederick State Park. A 560-acre park in nearby Maryland with a stone fort built in 1756 to protect settlers during the French and Indian War and Pontiac's Rebellion. It was used as a prison during the Revolutionary War. A skirmish was fought here during the Civil War.

Gettysburg National Military Park

97 Taneytown Road
Gettysburg, PA 17325
717-334-1124
website: www.nps.gov/gett/

The Battle of Gettysburg, fought in and around the small market town of Gettysburg from July 1 to July 3, 1863, turned out to be the "High Tide of the Confederacy," the farthest advance made by the rebelling Southerners into Northern territory. It resulted in a hard-won Union victory in which more than 51,000 soldiers on both sides were killed, wounded, or captured, making it the bloodiest battle of the Civil War. The three days of heavy fighting at Gettysburg, historians agree, were pivotal to the outcome of the Civil War. It was the largest battle of any war that has been fought in Pennsylvania and was responsible for more deaths and casualties than any other battle fought in North America.

The battle also marked the last major effort by Confedeate general Robert E. Lee to take the fighting out of Virginia and into the Northern states as he audaciously marched his large force into Pennsylvania. He had given his troops several weeks to recuperate after their hard-fought May 1863 victory at Chancellorsville in northern Virginia, in which the Southerners had outflanked and pushed back a numerically superior Northern army.

The Confederates had several sound reasons for undertaking this invasion of the North. Such a move would capitalize on the momentum generated by the victory at Chancellorsville. They also believed that an invasion and victory in the North would strengthen the hand of factions in the North who wanted to bring the war to an end. Perhaps President Abraham Lincoln could be persuaded to end the conflict through negotiation. Such an offensive, if successful, might also persuade England and France to recognize the South as an independent nation.

The invasion would have other benefits as well. It would force the Union Army to follow the Confederates northward, removing the Yankees from the South and relieving the threat to the Southern capital of Richmond. And by moving into Pennsylvania, Lee's army would be in

Reenactors Set the Historic Scene

For an event to really come to life at one of Pennsylvania's historic military sites, a personal ingredient is necessary: living-history reenactors who make it all seem real. As dedicated enthusiasts who are fascinated with history, these reenactors willingly forsake their modern-day lives and conveniences, don period uniforms, shoulder muskets, and transform themselves briefly into eighteenth-century American militiamen or nineteenth-century Civil War foot soldiers.

These volunteer "weekend warriors" spend their time setting up a campsite, portraying camp life, drilling as soldiers in the ranks, firing cannons or muskets, flying vintage aircraft, or taking part in a historic battle action. These history buffs bring reality to the historic event, helping to provide a better understanding of it, by peopling it with soldiers, sailors, and airmen like those who originally earned the site its place in history.

At the 135th anniversary of the Battle of Gettysburg in 1998, for example, the largest reenactment ever held in the United States, more than 17,000 battle reenactors and 5,000 civilian reenactors staged three days of battle action in the rolling countryside near where the original battle took place. Thousands of spectators watched as skirmishers formed battle lines and moved toward the enemy. Artillerymen maneuvered their cannons into place and fired to keep the foe at bay. Infantrymen formed tight ranks, then forged ahead, stopped, reloaded, and fired a mass volley. Officers wheeled their horses, urging them from one end of the battle line to the other. Medics tended the wounded, while mounted messengers galloped from unit to unit, coordinating their commanders' orders. Young drummer boys lugged canvas water bags to quench the thirst of the fighting men. Smoke hung over the battlefield during the three days of battle.

Members of reenactment units travel from battlefield to battlefield, forming up for each weekend's scheduled events. For the next several days, they take on the character of the soldiers they portray, right down

enemy territory and therefore free to commandeer food, horses, and supplies. Many of these needed supplies were no longer available in the South because of the continuous fighting there and because of the effects of the Union blockade that prevented ships from reaching Southern ports.

The Confederacy's gray columns trooped northward up the Shenandoah Valley, across the Potomac River into Maryland, through the to the muddy boots, wet bedrolls, and a fitful night's sleep. Often it's a family affair with wives, sons, and daughters dressed in period clothing tending the campfire, cooking the evening meal, and gathering wood and water. Enthusiasts of the Civil War make up the largest group of such battle actors, but other eras have their participants as well. Some portray British or American soldiers of the Revolutionary War; others become Indians or frontiersmen of the French and Indian War, sailors in the Spanish-American War, or soldiers, sailors, or airmen of World War I or World War II.

Gen. Winfield Scott Hancock is personified by Bruce Stocking of the National Park Service. Stocking and his wife have also led a move to restore the Civil War general's mausoleum at Montgomery Cemetery in Norristown. Some reenactors gain a reputation for their first-person roles, while others become members of fighting units.

Such reenacting of historic moments got a big boost in 1961 with a large-scale event that commemorated the hundreth anniversary of the Civil War Battle of Manassas in Virginia. The Bicentennial of the American Revolution in 1976 spurred new enthusiasm, as did the fiftieth anniversary commemorations of World War II in the 1990s.

Every battle reenactment needs soldiers of both sides. At the annual Battle of Bushy Run, bare-chested Indians in authentic war paint harass the British redcoats. At the yearly Battle of Brandywine, British regulars repel George Washington's Continental Army. Confederate soldiers fight the Union troops every five years at the Battle of

continued on page 150

Cumberland Valley, and into Pennsylvania, striking fear into Northern citizens. Maj. Gen. Jubal Early's Confederate forces extracted $28,000 in ransom from the city of York. Lt. Gen. Richard Ewell's forces captured Chambersburg and sent a division toward Harrisburg (see page 143), Pennsylvania's capital. Washington grew tense. Philadelphia was fearful.

Impelled by the crisis and dissatisfied with his commander in the field, President Abraham Lincoln relieved Gen. Joseph Hooker. Every-

Gettysburg. At the annual Battle of the Bulge, German storm troopers battle it out with Allied soldiers.

For a reenactor, such an event is more than just a weekend away from home; it's a challenge to "become" another person, to step back into another era. It's a time perhaps to follow in the footsteps of one's forebears, to appreciate what one's ancestor achieved, and to share those feelings with others. Bruce Stocking of Valley Forge has been a reenactor since his father took him to a Civil War battle when he was a teenager. Now he is often called upon to portray Maj. Gen. Winfield Scott Hancock, commander of the I and II Corps at the Battle of Gettysburg. So caught up is Stocking in his part-time role that he and his wife, Karen, have even taken it upon themselves to restore and maintain the mausoleum of the Civil War general, who is buried in Montgomery Cemetery in Norristown.

If you are interested in becoming a reenactor, regional and local units are always looking for new members. It is estimated that some 25,000 Civil War reenactors are currently active, as well as hundreds more who rep-

Charles Morrison of Garner, North Carolina (left), portrays a fighting Civil War chaplain of the 6th North Carolina Infantry who not only ministered to wounded soldiers but also shouldered a rifle. At a reenactment at Gettysburg, he stands with his twelve-year-old grandson, Christopher Burcar (center), and twelve-year-old nephew, Matthew Meadows. True to their characters, they do not smile for the camera.

one knew that the Union Army would soon have to do battle to stop the Confederate advance. Desperate for a general who would aggressively combat the Rebels, Lincoln lost no time in appointing Gen. George G. Meade, a Pennsylvanian, to command the Union forces at this critical juncture.

resent other periods of history. Many of them got started by attending a historic reenactment and talking with the seasoned reenactors themselves. Although there is no central organization for the living-history groups, reenactors are usually glad to help steer a newcomer to a nearby unit. As one example, Company C of the 28th Pennsylvania Volunteer Infantry meets regularly at the Civil War Museum and Library in Philadelphia.

Guy LaFrance and Laura Davis, both of Manassas, Virginia, portray a Union soldier of the 3rd U.S. Infantry and his wife at a reenactment at Gettysburg.

There are, however, a few other sources that may help you find your niche in this rewarding pastime. For the Revolutionary War, you can get further information about units and reenactment events from the Brigade of the American Revolution, 531 Westward Avenue, Rivervale, NJ 17675-5526. A monthly newspaper covers all living-history periods and supplies participants with event dates and other news of reenactments units. Write to *Smoke and Fire News*, P.O. Box 166, Grand Rapids, OH 43522, or call 419-832-0303. A monthly magazine lists upcoming Civil War events and carries advertisements of uniforms, firearms, and equipment needed by the historical hobbyist. Write to *Camp Chase Gazette*, P.O. Box 707, Marietta, OH 45750-0707, or call 800-449-1865 or 740-373-1865.

On the Internet, use the keyword "Reenactors" to lead you to "History for Today." Under this heading, you can browse among reenactment units listed by state, including "Historical Groups in Pennsylvania." The Yahoo search engine also lists many items under the search heading "Reenactors," including home pages for individual units, organizations, and publications such as the *Camp Chase Gazette*. ∎

Although taken by surprise by the appointment, Meade assumed command of the army and followed Lee northward, staying well to the east, where he could keep his troops between the Confederate Army and the capital at Washington. Lee had detached Maj. Gen. J. E. B. Stuart and his cavalry from the main Confederate forces so they could

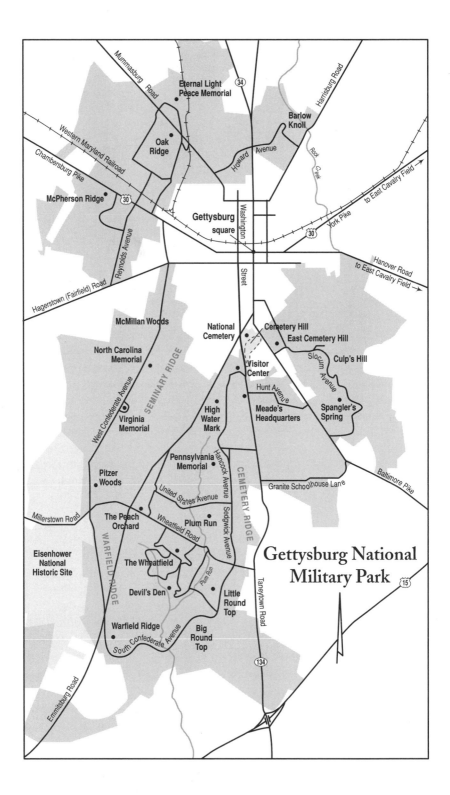

Gettysburg National
Military Park

Soldiers from the 5th Michigan Infantry Regiment march through their Union camp during one of the large-scale battle reenactments that take place at Gettysburg.

operate independently and seize needed supplies from the countryside. But without Stuart's cavalry, the Southern commander was late in learning of Meade's appointment, and it was not until June 30 that Lee learned that the Northern forces were following him into Pennsylvania with a 90,000-man army.

Lee immediately ordered his own scattered army totaling 75,000 to come together in the Gettysburg area at the town of Cashtown, consolidating the various units of the Confederate force that had marched northward along different routes.

The two armies collided on July 1, 1863, when a Confederate foray into the town of Gettysburg ran into a Union cavalry brigade. Both armies were ready for a fight; Gettysburg just happened to be the unplanned location where this major battle would take place. Gettysburg was like the hub of a wheel, with no less than ten roads and turnpikes radiating from this small farming town. Oddly enough, when the armies met, the Confederates moved in from the north and west, while the Union forces approached from the south and east. The countryside around Gettysburg was flat and open, covered with farm fields and rolling hills, and interspersed with woods.

WHAT YOU SEE TODAY

Gettysburg National Military Park was established by Congress in 1895 to preserve the scene of this decisive battle and to memorialize the soldiers who fought there. The park incorporates more than 5,700 acres and includes 30 miles of park roads, 147 historic buildings, and more than 1,400 monuments, markers, and memorials. More than 1.8 million people visit the park each year, including many from other countries.

Visitors Center. When visiting the battlefield, go first to the visitors center, where park rangers will help tailor your visit and sell you entrance tickets for certain sites, including the later farm home of President Dwight Eisenhower, which is located adjacent to the battlefield. Also in the visitors center are orientation displays; extensive exhibits of Civil War arms, equipment, and uniforms; current schedules of ranger-conducted programs; and a bookstore that contains a wide selection of Civil War books, videos, and photographs. During the summer, park rangers offer a variety of talks, walks, living-history presentations, and children's programs. The Electric Map presentation at the visitors center gives a narrative of the three-day battle, as colored lights flash to pinpoint sites on a large model of the battlefield terrain. Adults $3, seniors $2, children $1.

Battlefield Trails. The best way to sense the land and the slower pace of Gettysburg's past is to walk the battlefield, as thousands of soldiers once did. The High Water Mark Trail, about a mile long, begins at the Cyclorama Center and leads past regimental monuments, stone breastworks, part of an artillery battery, the ground defended by Union soldiers in repulsing Pickett's Charge, and General Meade's headquarters. The trail takes about an hour to walk. For a longer hike, inquire about the 9-mile Billy Yank Trail or the 3.5-mile Johnny Reb Trail. Besides these trails, there are paths to Devil's Den and the Point of Woods, as well as a self-guided tour of the National Cemetery.

Cyclorama Center. Contains exhibits, a free film, and the 360-foot Gettysburg Cyclorama, a semicircular painting of Pickett's Charge, by Paul Philippoteaux, displayed as part of a sound-and-light program inside a large, circular auditorium. The unique building, which has won architectural awards, was constructed in 1962 to display the 356-foot-long painting. Adults $3.00, seniors and children, $2.00.

Sites of the First Day's Battle

On the first day of the 3-day battle, elements of the two armies collided during the early-morning hours. The fighting escalated throughout the day, as more Union and Confederate troops reached the field. By 4 P.M., the defending Federal troops were defeated and retreated through Gettysburg, where many were captured. The remnants of the Union forces fell back and regrouped on Cemetery Hill and Culp's Hill. The action during the first day took place primarily northwest of town. Ridges, creeks, woodlots and farm fields, buildings, and roads determined where the battle actions took place.

As the Confederate forces approached Gettysburg along the Chambersburg Pike from the west, the Union Army staked out a defensive position along McPherson Ridge. This ridge, really a gentle rise in the terrain, lies a scant mile northwest of the town square in Gettysburg.

Maj. Gen. John Reynolds, a veteran army officer who was born in Lancaster, Pennsylvania, took charge of rallying the Union forces and getting them into position to defend the ridge. Reynolds's orderly described what happened next: "He ordered [the 19th Indiana Regiment] 'forward into line' at a double quick and ordered them to charge into the woods, leading the charge in person. The regiment charged into the woods nobly, but the enemy was too strong, and they [the Union forces] had to give way to the right. The enemy pushed on, and was now not much more than 60 paces from where the General was. Minie balls were flying thick. The General turned to look towards the seminary [the nearby Lutheran Theological Seminary] . . . to see if other troops were coming on and as he did so a minie ball struck him in the back of the neck and he fell from his horse dead." Thus fell one of the Union's ablest and most popular commanders, killed by what was probably a sharpshooter's bullet early on the first day of the battle. His soldiers carried his body from the field in a blanket swung between their muskets.

Furious fighting ensued as the two armies clashed. Artillery shells ripped through the woods that covered part of the ridge. At one point, Union forces took as prisoners 250 Confederate soldiers who found themselves trapped in a railway cut with no means of escape.

At the northern end of McPherson Ridge, an area called Oak Ridge, the Federals took cover behind one of the stone walls that separate farm fields in the area. From their protected position, the riflemen

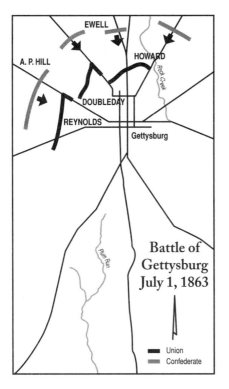

EWELL

A. P. HILL

HOWARD

Rock Creek

DOUBLEDAY

REYNOLDS

Gettysburg

Plum Run

Battle of Gettysburg July 1, 1863

■ Union
▨ Confederate

cut down hundreds of North Carolinians trying to advance across an open field. "Unable to advance, unwilling to retreat," the North Carolina troops were slaughtered or taken prisoner. Every commissioned officer of the 23rd North Carolina Regiment except one was either killed or wounded.

Both sides brought up reinforcements. After more furious fighting, the Confederates succeeded in blasting their way through Herbst Woods, a wooded portion of the ridge. "The lines were pouring volleys into each other at a distance not greater than 20 paces," one survivor reported. Union troops fell back all along the line, with a strong delaying action being fought by Pennsylvania regiments known as the Bucktails, expert riflemen from the state's mountain region who had attached buck deer tails to their caps. Today's traveler approaching Gettysburg from the west on the Chambersburg Road sees the figure of a Pennsylvania mountaineer holding his rifle musket. The statue is positioned at the "hot corner" of the first day's battle, where the Pennsylvanians held their ground for 5 hours before giving way to superior Confederate forces.

In the afternoon, the Union forces found themselves outnumbered and outflanked. They were ordered to fall back through town and take up new positions to defend Cemetery Hill, which rose 100 feet above the southern edge of the town and overlooked three key roads. Confused crowds of soldiers tried to move through the streets as other units entered town. Streets were jammed with military vehicles, horses, and troops. Some 500 Union soldiers were captured by the pursuing Confederates.

But the Confederate forces had had enough after a hard-fought day and returned at dusk to encampments set up behind Seminary Ridge. Meanwhile, the Federals reorganized their units and occupied the high ground at Culp's Hill and Cemetery Hill. They spent the night fortifying their positions. "All night long the busy axes from tens of thousands of busy hands on that crest rang out clearly on the night air and bespoke the preparation the enemy were making for the morrow," wrote a Confederate junior officer who could hear the Union activity across the way.

WHAT YOU SEE TODAY

Oak Ridge. A number of monuments to soldiers from Pennsylvania, Massachusetts, New York, and Wisconsin line Doubleday Avenue and Buford Avenue, the park roads that follow this ridgeline, the scene of the first day's battle. The monuments are reminders of the stubborn fight made by the Union infantry units against superior Confederate numbers before the Federals were forced to fall back through town.

McPherson Ridge. Reynolds Avenue traces this ridgeline. This area is still thick woods, as it was at the time of the conflict.

Statue of Maj. Gen. John Reynolds. This equestrian statue, raised with money collected by officers and men of Reynolds's brigade, honors the highest-ranking Union general killed at Gettysburg. It is made from bronze melted from captured Confederate cannons, a tribute to one of the most able and popular commanders in the Union Army. A smaller monument nearby, erected by the state of Pennsylvania, marks the spot when General Reynolds was killed.

Eternal Light Peace Memorial. This monument is the result of a concerted effort of 50,000 Union and Confederate veterans of the war, who gathered at Gettysburg in 1913 to construct a monument to peace and unity within the nation. In 1938, on the 75th anniversary of the battle, President Franklin D. Roosevelt dedicated the 40-foot-high memorial. Two thousand aging Civil War veterans attended the ceremony, part of a crowd of 250,000 spectators. The gas flame atop the monument burns continuously.

Sites of the Second Day's Battle

Further reinforcements arrived for both sides during the night and early morning of the second day. The main strength of both armies had now arrived for what both generals knew would be a major battle. By midmorning, 65,000 Confederates were on the field facing 85,000 Union soldiers.

By morning, the Union Army was dug into well-fortified positions along the low ridgeline of Cemetery Ridge. The Union line was shaped

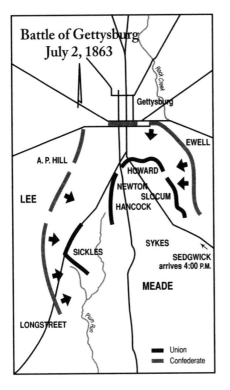

Battle of Gettysburg
July 2, 1863

Rock Creek

Gettysburg

EWELL

A. P. HILL

HOWARD

NEWTON

LEE

SLOCUM

HANCOCK

SYKES

SICKLES

SEDGWICK
arrives 4:00 P.M.

MEADE

LONGSTREET

Plum Run

■■ Union
■■ Confederate

in the form of an upside-down fishhook, with the hook at Culp's Hill and Cemetery Hill at the northern end, and Big Round Top and Little Round Top Hills located at the southern end. At this point, General Meade replaced Maj. Gen. Oliver Howard with Maj. Gen. Winfield Scott Hancock as the principal field leader of the Federal forces.

General Lee envisioned coordinated attacks by his Southerners on the Union defenders. One would hit the Union left at the two promontories of Little Round Top and Big Round Top, while the other would assault the Union right based on Culp's Hill and Cemetery Hill. These attacks came in the late afternoon. However, the two thrusts were not made simultaneously, as Lee wanted, but were two hours apart. As a result, General Meade was able to shift Union troops from one end of his line to the other, and the Federals were able to turn back both attacks.

First came the attack on Big Round Top and Little Round Top by a corps under the command of Lt. Gen. James Longstreet, one of Lee's most reliable generals. A Confederate force captured Big Round Top after a heroic climb to the crest over huge boulders and around bushes in the face of heavy sniper fire. But when the Confederates moved against nearby Little Round Top, they ran into furious fire from the Federals, who had commanded the summit. Often the two lines surged so close together that the troops did not have time to load their muskets but were forced to fight with bayonets, gun butts, and even rocks. Finally, a bayonet charge by soldiers from the 20th Maine Regiment, led by Col. Joshua Chamberlain, drove the Confederates off the hill and prevented the left end of the Union line from being flanked.

In other fighting nearby, savage combat raged through places later remembered by history: the Peach Orchard, the Wheatfield, Devil's

Den, and the Valley of Death. A private from Massachusetts later vividly remembered the sounds of the action: "The hoarse and indistinguishable orders of commanding officers, the screaming and bursting of shells, canister and shrapnel as they tore through the struggling masses of humanity, the death screams of wounded animals, the groans of their human companions, wounded and dying trampled underfoot by hurrying batteries, riderless horses, and the moving lines of battle . . . a perfect hell on earth, never, perhaps, to be equaled, certainly not to be surpassed, nor ever to be forgotten in a man's lifetime."

Late in the day, the Confederates made their attack at the northern end of the Union line, attaining the top of Cemetery Hill, beating back the Union defenders, and destroying several Union cannons. Shifting units from other parts of the line, the Union forces managed to contain the Confederate breakthrough. In the gathering darkness, the soldiers in blue threw back the men in gray, who were forced to retreat down the hill in the moonlight leaving Cemetery Hill once more under the control of the Union forces.

WHAT YOU SEE TODAY

Pitzer Woods and Warfield Ridge. From the treeline of Pitzer Woods, at the southern end of Seminary Ridge, Confederate troops mounted assaults against Union troops that were occupying Devil's Den, the Wheatfield, the Peach Orchard, Little Round Top, and Big Round Top. Today monuments to troops from North Carolina, Tennessee, Virginia, Florida, Louisiana, Mississippi, Georgia, South Carolina, Arkansas, Texas, and Alabama dot West Confederate Avenue, which traces these Confederate positions.

Devil's Den. This name was given to a cluster of huge granite boulders near the foot of Big Round Top. After the Confederates pushed Union troops from this jumble of rocks, Southern sharpshooters hid here and picked off Federal officers and soldiers on Little Round Top. Visitors today view the scene much as it appeared in 1863.

The Wheatfield. Hay grows now in the open fields where charges and countercharges by both sides strewed this area and the nearby woods with the bodies of more than 4,000 dead and wounded. At the end of the fighting, Southern forces had control of the plain in front of Cemetery Ridge, including the Wheatfield, but the Union forces held the high ground of Cemetery Ridge behind it.

The Peach Orchard. Peach trees have been planted again by the park to replicate the Civil War scene. Here, Federal troops who took positions on the open ground in front of Cemetery Ridge were overrun by the Confederates.

Little Round Top. The tour road leads to the top of this tree-covered hill that played an important tactical role in the day's battle. The Union sent in reinforcements to man this high point after Maj. Gen. Daniel Sickles moved his troops forward to the Wheatfield and Peach Orchard. Numerous monuments attest to the heavy fighting that resulted in the Union forces remaining in control of the hill.

Pennsylvania State Memorial. The largest monument on the battlefield, this domed structure is made of granite (see front cover). On the parapet that forms its base are bronze tablets bearing the names of all the soldiers from Pennsylvania who fought at Gettysburg. Eight portrait statues represent President Lincoln, Gov. Andrew Curtin, and six key Pennsylvania generals: Maj. Gen. George Meade, Maj. Gen. John Reynolds, Maj. Gen. Winfield Scott Hancock, Maj. Gen. David Birney, Maj. Gen. Alfred Pleasonton, and Brig. Gen. David Gregg. In all, sixty-nine infantry regiments, nine cavalry regiments, seven artillery batteries, and fifteen generals from Pennsylvania took part in the battle. Of the 34,530 Pennsylvanians who were present, 1,182 were killed or mortally wounded and 3,177 were wounded.

Sites of the Third Day's Battle

The third, and critical, day's fighting opened before daybreak with the unfinished business of the day before at Culp's Hill, where the Confederates still half encircled the Union position. Confederate soldiers attacked in the early-morning light; Union soldiers fought them off and countercharged. After three more hours of renewed heavy fighting, the exhausted Confederates withdrew. As an indication of the severity of the battle, one Union brigade counted 500 dead on its battlefront alone.

Now an eerie calm settled over the entire battlefield, as all engagements were temporarily halted. Back at his headquarters, General Lee was determined to generate one last effort to break the Union lines. At 1 P.M., Confederate artillery batteries, some 130 guns, opened up. Union artillery, some 80 guns, replied. Thus commenced "one of the grandest artillery duels in the history of wars." It was a severe testing for the Union soldiers. Maj. Gen. Carl Schurz called the bombardment of heavy artillery "one of the hardest trials of the courage and steadfastness of the soldier. . . . It bewilders the mind of the bravest with a painful sense of helplessness against tremendous power."

After an hour, the Federal artillery ceased firing, partly to save ammunition and partly to trick the Confederates into believing that their intense bombardment had silenced the Union guns. As the Confederate artillery continued to fire, some 12,000 Southern infantrymen of Lt. Gen. James Longstreet's I Corps emerged from the woods of Seminary Ridge. In the center was Maj. Gen. George Pickett's division, which had arrived on the battlefield only the day before. Alongside Pickett's division were the regiments of Maj. Gen. James Pettigrew and Maj. Gen. Isaac Trimble.

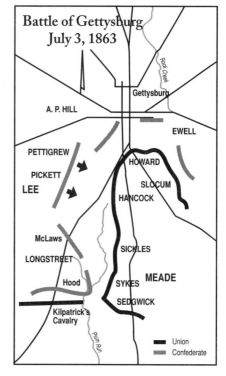

Row upon row, the gray-uniformed soldiers marched forward, flags waving, bayonets flashing in the sunlight, in what became known as Pickett's Charge. Led by their officers, a few mounted on horseback, the soldiers marched in ranks across the gently sloping fields toward the Union defenders, who were strung out along Cemetery Ridge behind a 2-foot-high stone wall that paralleled Emmitsburg Road.

The center of the Union line, which bore the brunt of the attack, was under the field command of Maj. Gen. Winfield Scott Hancock and consisted of Maj. Gen. John Gibbons's II Corps and Maj. Gen. John Newton's I Corps. A full mile of open fields lay between the Confederate attackers and the Union entrenchments.

Before they had traversed more than a few hundred yards, the Southerners discovered that the Union artillery was far from silenced. As canisters of grapeshot and shrapnel were hurled into the advancing troops, great gaps were torn in the ranks as men and horses fell. But other soldiers quickly filled the gaps, and the lines came on unwaveringly. "We could not help hitting them at every shot," said a Union artillery officer.

Behind their protecting stone wall, the Union infantrymen continued to hold their fire, watching with fascination as the mass of Confed-

Smoke drifts across the battlefield as Union troops defend their lines during a reenactment of the third day of the Battle of Gettysburg.

erates moved steadily toward them. Finally, when their opponents were fewer than 100 yards away, there came the order to fire. A barrage of cannon and musket fire went off at once. The attackers were enveloped in a dense cloud of smoke and dust. "Arms, heads, blankets, guns and knapsacks were tossed into the clear air," an officer said. "A moan went up from the field."

"Seconds are centuries, minutes ages. Men fire into each other's faces not five feet apart," one survivor wrote. "There are bayonet thrusts, saber strokes, pistol shots . . . men going down on their hands and knees, spinning round like tops, throwing out their arms, gulping blood, falling, legless, armless, headless. There are ghastly heaps of dead men."

Only a few hundred Confederates reached the stone wall. At the height of the attack, Major General Hancock, astride his horse, was shot—a wound he suffered from the rest of his life. The Union's line was broken and driven back, but it reformed and, with the aid of troops from both right and left flanks, slowly regained its superiority. At the Angle, where the fieldstone wall used for defense by the Union soldiers takes a sharp jog, shot, shell, canister, and musketry combined in intense fighting. Battle flags dropped. Confederates threw up their hands and surrendered.

"The Southern lines waver," a newspaper correspondent wrote. "The soldiers of the front rank look round for their supports. They are gone—fleeing over the field, broken, shattered, thrown into confusion by the remorseless fire. . . . Thousands of rebels throw down their arms and give themselves up as prisoners."

Meanwhile, the Confederate cavalry had circled around behind the Union lines, as Lee had planned (see sidebar on page 164), but was turned back by Union cavalry after a hard-fought battle at East Cavalry Field and, therefore, failed to attack the Union forces from the rear.

Lee rode out to meet the infantry survivors who straggled back. "It's all my fault," he told them. In all, 6,500 men had fallen or been captured, half of those who marched so proudly out of the woods. All fifteen regimental commanders had been hit; so had seventeen field officers, three brigadier generals, and eight colonels.

The dead lie, one New Jersey soldier wrote "upon the open fields, in crevices of the rocks, behind fences, trees and buildings; in thickets, where they had crept for safety only to die in agony; by stream or wall or hedge, wherever the battle had raged or their weakening steps could carry them."

Badly beaten, Lee was forced to retreat southward the next day. The Federals followed, but they were too exhausted to mount a vigorous pursuit, and the Confederates were able to cross the Potomac River back into familiar territory. The army that staggered into Virginia was physically exhausted. Never again would Lee attempt an offensive operation of such magnitude. And Meade, through criticized for not pursuing Lee's troops, would forever be remembered as the man who won the battle that has come to be known as the "high water mark of the Confederacy." After this invasion, the Confederates were never again able to threaten in the North in force, and they were on the defensive for the remaining two years of the war.

WHAT YOU SEE TODAY

Virginia State Memorial. Clearly visible to visitors across the open fields that were crossed by the Confederate infantrymen during Pickett's Charge, this memorial is one of the largest monuments on the battlefield. From this spot, General Lee watched the assault. The memorial was the first of the Southern state monuments to be erected on the battlefield. Park rangers often start tours describing Pickett's Charge from the Virginia Memorial.

High Water Mark. This stone monument marks the farthest advance of the Confederates who assaulted the Union lines during Pickett's Charge. The "copse of trees" referred to in Lee's orders to his troops as a reference point still grows here. The monument consists of an open book of granite supported by two pyramids of cannonballs. On

Union Repels Confederate Cavalry

A wild card in the high stakes tactical contest of the third day's battle at Gettysburg was the Confederate cavalry under the command of Maj. Gen. J. E. B. Stuart. Stuart had his orders from General Lee to try to outflank the Union Army anchored at the fishhook on Culp's Hill and attack the vulnerable rear of the defending Northern infantry. If the mass attack called Pickett's Charge had succeeded in breaking through the defending Union lines, Stuart's mounted troops could have created havoc among the Federal soldiers by trapping them in a deadly vise. If that had happened, the Battle of Gettysburg might have come to a dramatically different conclusion.

Events, however, dictated a far different outcome. While the heavy artillery battle was thundering 2 miles to the west, Stuart and his force of 3,500 cavalrymen and horse-drawn artillerymen began their move to swing around the end of the Union lines, hoping they would not be spotted by Union scouts.

But they were spotted. Thus warned, the Union cavalry chief, Brig. Gen. David Gregg, immediately moved his Union force of 5,000 cavalrymen and artillery into a position to block Stuart's advance. Gregg was another Pennsylvanian, born in Huntingdon.

The two cavalry forces collided in the partly wooded farming countryside in the early afternoon of July 3. Stuart hid his cavalrymen in the woods atop a ridge that overlooked open farm fields. To open the battle, dismounted Confederate riflemen appeared from behind the protection of a barn, formed a skirmish line, and attacked the Federal force that faced them. To back up the skirmishers, Stuart then sent mounted troopers across the fields to drive back the Union cavalry. At the same time, Confederate cannoneers fired at the Union

the pages of the book are the names of the Confederate units that participated in the assault and the Union units that repulsed it. Nearby is the Angle; some Confederate soldiers reached this point and battled the defenders in hand-to-hand combat before they were subdued.

Statue of Gen. George G. Meade. Located near the High Water Mark, this equestrian statue honors the man who not only won this crucial battle, but also successfully led the army through the next two years of war. The statue stands at the spot where General Meade rode up shortly after the failure of Pickett's Charge and received the jubilant troops. The Union cavalrymen repelled both the skirmishers and the mounted cavalry charge, making good use of a new repeating rifle some of them had recently been issued.

In the late afternoon, Stuart, from his sanctuary in the woods, launched the last great mounted charge of the day—a thrust with 1,900 horsemen. "As the charge was ordered the speed increased, every horse on the jump, every man yelling like a demon," a Union officer recalled. "As the opposing columns drew nearer and nearer, each with perfect alignment, every man gathered his horse well under him and gripped his weapon the tighter."

In reaction, the Union cavalry charged into the Confederates from three sides and broke their formations in bloody hand-to-hand combat. A Confederate officer described the fighting as "hand-to-hand, blow for blow, cut for cut, oath for oath. It seems as if the very furies from the infernal regions were turned loose on each other."

Unable to withstand the furious attack upon their front and flanks, the Confederates soon retreated to the wooded ridgeline. After almost two hours of fighting, the battle had been decided. Stuart, with his route around the Union lines blocked, could not carry out the rest of his plan to attack the unsuspecting Union forces from the rear. Gregg, although outnumbered, was able to stubbornly resist the best the Southern cavalry could throw at him. In the battle, the Union lost 254 men killed, wounded, and missing, and the Confederates lost 181.

The Union had successfully turned back the vaunted Confederate cavalry, strengthening the growing reputation of the Union cavalry as a fighting outfit. It had prevented Stuart from outflanking the Union's fishhook battleline and nullified the Confederate strategy that might have coordinated a cavalry charge by Stuart with a breakthrough of the Northern lines by the infantry—a plan that might have brought the Southerners victory instead of defeat at Gettysburg. ■

shouts of his victorious soldiers. Fittingly, the Meade statue faces the statue of General Lee at the Virginia Memorial across almost a mile of open fields.

Meade's Headquarters. General Meade directed the battle action and on the evening of July 2 held a council of war in the white clapboard farmhouse owned by Lydia Leister on Taneytown Road. The original house still stands today. An observer at the council in 1863 recalled that the Union generals who gathered "were as calm, mild-mannered and free from flurry or excitement as a board of commissioners meeting to discuss a street improvement." Later, during the third day's battle, however, Meade was driven from the house by the intense Confederate artillery bombardment.

East Cavalry Field. Before you visit this detached area of the park, obtain an information sheet on East Cavalry Field at the park visitors center. From the traffic circle in the center of Gettysburg, follow PA Route 116 east 3.5 miles to the brown-and-white sign labeled "East Cavalry Field." A 2-mile self-guided tour road takes you past sites that commemorate one of the largest cavalry battles of the war, with interpretive signs at four stops. The scene appears much the same as at the time of the battle. A farmhouse and barn still stand where the Rummel farm stood in 1863. Cress Ridge remains covered with trees, as it was then. The open fields suitable for a cavalry charge still stretch along the tour road. Civil War cannons stand where Union and Confederate batteries blasted at each other. The only difference seems to be the monuments that mark the battlefield. The Michigan Cavalry Brigade Monument, which honors Brig. Gen. George Custer and his Michigan cavalrymen, is the largest monument on the field. This 40-foot-high granite monument was dedicated by survivors of the brigade in 1889. Several hundred yards away is the Gregg Cavalry Shaft, erected in 1884, commemorating both the Union and Confederate cavalrymen who battled on the field.

Gettysburg National Cemetery

On a brisk November day, four months after the battle that had left 8,000 Union and Confederate dead lying in the fields, a new cemetery to hold the bodies of the Union soldiers was dedicated.

A large procession wound its way from Gettysburg's main square through town streets to the new burial ground, an area that abutted the older civilian Evergreen Cemetery. Platoons of Union soldiers and a military band preceded fifty or more horses that bore the dignitaries, including President Abraham Lincoln, many of Lincoln's Cabinet members, and Gov. Andrew Curtin of Pennsylvania. The dignitaries dismounted at Evergreen Cemetery's gatehouse, which still bears scars from bullets and shells fired during the battle for Cemetery Hill.

A small speakers' stand had been built to face a large semicircle of graves that formed the central portion of the new national cemetery. Within the semicircle, the graves were arranged by states. Only one-third of the burials had yet been completed.

A crowd of about 15,000 pressed closely toward the platform so the people could hear the speakers. The main oration was given by Edward Everett, a former secretary of state, now president of Harvard College, who held the attention of the crowd for nearly two hours, recounting the battle and praising the victors. When Everett finished, President Lincoln was introduced to dedicate the cemetery. Acknowledged today as one of the great speeches of history, Lincoln's Gettyburg Address has given inspiration to democratic leaders around the world ever since. With this speech, Lincoln accomplished the mission he had come to Gettysburg for, raising the spirits of the Northerners, who now realized that the destructive Civil War would not end soon. He transformed the tragedy of dead soldiers into a sacrifice for the proposition that "all men are created equal" under the U.S. Constitution.

Once the cemetery had been dedicated, the task remained to rebury hundreds of Union soldiers. After the battle, teams of soldiers, Confederate prisoners, and townspeople had done their best to identify the thousands of corpses. They had hastily buried the bodies in shallow graves on the battlefield and posted crude grave markers that contained only sketchy information. These graves had deteriorated in the hot, humid summer weather. In the bitterness of the Civil War, most of the Confederate dead continued to lie in temporary graves for months or years until family members or state delegations retrieved them for proper burial in the South. Following the war, the remains of 3,320 Confederate soldiers were removed from Gettysburg to cemeteries in Richmond and other Southern cities.

The Soldier's National Monument was the first of many memorials to be placed in the National Cemetery at Gettysburg. White marble figures surrounding the base represent War, History, Plenty, and Peace.

To the townspeople, it seemed as though the whole village of Gettysburg and its surroundings had become one makeshift burial ground. To cope with this emotional situation, Governor Curtin appointed David Wills as his agent to organize a permanent burial place. Wills formed an interstate commission to collect funds to bury the Union dead. The fourteen states involved were assessed according to their representation in Congress. The federal government provided the caskets, shipping thousands to Gettysburg.

The 17-acre site chosen was part of one of the primary battlesites of the second day's fighting—Cemetery Hill—and adjoined Evergreen Cemetery. The new cemetery was designed by a well-known rural architect, William Saunders. Since Saunders did not know how many bodies from which states would need to be buried, he conceived the semicircular design, which would be flexible enough to accommodate varying numbers. Within the semicircle, burials were arranged by state.

Many bodies were difficult to identify and sort into their proper military units. Soldiers whose home states could not be ascertained, even though their names were known, were buried with the "unknowns." Reburial of 3,555 bodies of Union soldiers began October 27 and took several months.

WHAT YOU SEE TODAY

Gettysburg National Cemetery. A half-mile self-guided walk leads visitors through what is one of the first national cemeteries. In season, park rangers conduct tours of the grounds. In addition to the dead from the Battle of Gettysburg, U.S. veterans from the Spanish-American War to the Vietnam War are also buried in the cemetery. It is the final resting place for more than 6,000 honorably discharged veterans and their dependents. Several Union Army cannons flank the tour road. The guns represent the fact that for three July days in 1863, Federal gunners fought the Confederates from this treeless hill.

The grave plots are arranged in a large semicircle surrounding the Soldiers' National Monument. The name and unit of each soldier are marked on his stone. The graves of some 979 unknown Union soldiers are marked with a numbered marble block. A handful of Confederate soldiers lie buried in the cemetery, testimony to the difficulty of identifying individual corpses on the battlefield.

Lincoln Speech Memorial. This is one of the few monuments ever erected to honor a speech rather than an individual. On the left side of the monument is an impression of the letter that Gettysburg attorney David Wills wrote inviting President Lincoln to speak at the dedication.

A bust of Lincoln stands in the center, with an engraving of the Gettysburg Address at the right. Behind the Lincoln Speech Memorial are some of the 3,307 post–Civil War grave sites. The imposing monument is not located precisely where Lincoln stood when he delivered his address. It was erected in 1912 at a site its sponsors thought fit the press reports of the event. Later research, however, based on two photographs of the dedication ceremony, disclosed that Lincoln spoke from a spot that is now within the neighboring Evergreen Cemetery.

Soldiers' National Monument. The first monument of any type to be placed at Gettysburg, this was part of the conception of architect William Saunders. It is the largest monument in the cemetery and honors all the Union dead. Consisting of a pedestal and shaft of white granite, it includes five statues fashioned of Italian marble.

Jennie Wade's Grave. Nearby, in the Evergreen Cemetery, is the grave of Mary Virginia "Jennie" Wade, killed by a sniper's bullet during the battle. Remarkably, she was the only civilian gunshot death reported during the three days of fighting. A U.S. flag flies from a pole over the grave site.

When to visit: The visitors center is open daily from 8 A.M. to 5 P.M. (6 P.M. in summer) except for Thanksgiving, Christmas, and New Year's Day. Park roads are open from 6 A.M. until 10 P.M. year-round. Visitation is highest from April to October.

Admission fees: No entrance fee for the park.

Special events: Memorial Day: ceremony and parade in the National Cemetery; mid-May to mid-October: Living-history programs and reenactors portraying military life; last weekend of June through first week of July: Civil War Heritage Days, including a living-history encampment, a Civil War reenactment with thousands of troops, a collectors show, a book fair, an antique arms show, and tours of Gettysburg; last week of June and first week of July: Civil War Institute, in which noted historians give lectures on Civil War topics; Saturday closest to November 19: ceremony commemorating the anniversary of Lincoln's Gettysburg Address.

Tours of the site: Self-guided battlefield road tours and audio cassette tapes available at the visitors center; two-hour guided tours with a licensed battlefield guide: $30 for up to five people, $45 for six to fifteen people.

Time needed to visit: At least one full day to tour the battlefield, visit the museum, view the Electric Map and Cyclorama, and take part in seasonal ranger-led activities.

Special considerations: The visitors center and Cyclorama Center are handicapped accessible, with at least one wheelchair at each building. Handicapped designated parking is available upon request. Pick up an accessibility brochure at the information desk.

Parking: Free parking in several lots, although considerable walking may be necessary when lots near the visitors center are filled.

Gift shop: Civil War books, videos, maps, posters, clothing, and memorabilia.

Directions: Gettysburg is located at the junction of U.S. Route 30 and U.S. Route 15. From exit 17 of the Pennsylvania Turnpike, travel south 30 miles on U.S. Route 15 to exit for Steinwehr Avenue. Follow signs to the park.

Tourist information

Gettysburg Convention and Visitors Bureau, 35 Carlisle Street, Gettysburg, PA 17325, telephone 717-334-6274, fax 717-334-1166, website www.gettysburg.com.

Other nearby sites

Civil War Discovery Trail. A project of the Civil War Trust, 2101 Wilson Boulevard, Suite 1120, Arlington, VA 22201. The trail links more than 500 Civil War sites in twenty-eight states, including battlefields, historic homes, stops on the Underground Railroad, and plantations. To trace military campaigns or get information, call 888-CW-TRAIL or visit website www.civilwar.org. Descriptions and visitor information are available in the *Civil War Trust's Official Guide to the Civil War Discovery Trail.*

Eisenhower National Historic Site Adjacent to the military park lie the home and farm of Gen. Dwight D. Eisenhower, 34th president of the United States. Tickets for the site and a shuttle bus are available at the park visitors center. The home is furnished as it was when the Eisenhowers lived there.

Caledonia State Park. The Appalachian Trail runs through this 1,130-acre park. The huge charcoal furnace that began operation in 1837 was destroyed by Confederates under Gen. Jubal Early in June 1863. Confederate troops used the pastures for field hospitals during the Battle of Gettysburg. Today visitors see a reconstructed furnace and blacksmith shop. The park also has a golf course, swimming, camping, fishing, and summer theater. Located midway between Gettysburg and Chambersburg on U.S. Route 30.

OTHER
MILITARY
LANDMARKS
IN
PENNSYLVANIA

Carlisle Barracks

Public Affairs Office
U.S. Army War College
Carlisle Barracks, PA 17013-5234
717-245-4101
fax 717-245-3711
e-mail: awcc.cpa@awc.carlisle.army.mil
website: carlisle-www.army.mil.

Carlisle Barracks was destined from the beginning to become a supply depot—a dispersal point for equipment and munitions and a mobilization point for the soldiers who would fight Pennsylvania's battles. From its earliest days, it has been a training site for soldiers and officers. Its history as an army installation began in the early 1750s, when settlers who had moved west of the Susquehanna River into the Cumberland Valley erected a stockade fort on the site of present-day Carlisle, which was named for Carlisle, England, where some of its first settlers came from.

In 1757, two years after the defeat of the British forces of Gen. Edward Braddock by the Indians (see pages 25–28), the new settlers expressed increased concern about Indian attacks. To further protect the region, Col. John Stanwix established a garrison of regular British Army troops at Carlisle. He built entrenchments as defensive works and sent out armed detachments to protect the area farmers while they harvested their crops.

Carlisle soon became the strongest position held by the British Army west of the Susquehanna River and was rapidly becoming an important supply base for future expeditions pushing west. Using Carlisle as a mobilization point, the British in 1758 moved to reassert their authority after the Braddock defeat. From here they would send another expedition to capture Fort Duquesne from the French and thereby gain control of the vital Ohio and Allegheny River Valleys.

For the task, the British high command appointed Brig. Gen. John Forbes, who in turn appointed Col. Henry Bouquet of the Royal American Regiment as his second in command. Troops for the expedition gathered at Carlisle: 2,700 Pennsylvania militiamen under Col. John Armstrong and 1,600 redcoats in Col. Archibald Montgomery's 77th Highland Regiment, together with four companies of Royal Americans, colonists who had signed up as soldiers in the regular British Army. Col. George Washington, leading 600 Virginians, joined them en route.

During the seven months it took the Forbes-Bouquet expedition to reach Fort Duquesne, stopping to construct Fort Bedford and Fort Ligonier along the way, long wagon trains of supplies followed from the staging area at Carlisle, carrying supplies to the troops. The capture of Fort Duquesne (see pages 13–15) and its transformation into Fort Pitt gave the British their first stronghold west of the Allegheny Mountains. Carlisle continued to serve as the point from which to supply these troops as they defended the migration of settlers into the new West.

Five years later, Bouquet once again organized a force at Carlisle to quell trouble in the West. With 400 troops, he marched to relieve Fort Pitt when it was besieged by Indians during Pontiac's Rebellion, overcoming an Indian ambush and outwitting and defeating the Indians at the Battle of Bushy Run (see pages 103–7). Bouquet's soldiers then moved on to disperse the Indian attackers and rescue Fort Pitt.

When the American Revolution broke out, the Continental Army took advantage of the skilled armorers and artisans who had been hired by the British to work at Carlisle. So in 1776, the Continental Congress authorized Carlisle to be an ordnance center to supply its new army and patriotically renamed the post Washingtonburg. Its workers responded by manufacturing and repairing cannons, muskets, bayonets, cartridge boxes, swords, and harnesses for horses. Here also was organized the army's first artillery school. Carlisle holds the distinction of being the second-oldest U.S. Army post in the country, after West Point.

After the Revolutionary War was won and the United States was born, the newly organized federal government had trouble asserting its authority and collecting its taxes. In 1794, farmers in western Pennsylvania joined in the Whiskey Rebellion (see pages 118–22). President Washington used his new federal powers to enforce the law. He requested the states of Pennsylvania and New Jersey to mobilize their militias at Carlisle. Then the president took to the field, mounted his horse, and reviewed the force of 10,000 militiamen that would carry out a successful campaign to disperse the agitators and compel the lawful payment of the back-due taxes. This was the first and only time a sitting president of the United States led an army of troops in the field.

During the 1800s, Carlisle Barracks became largely a training center and recruiting depot. Many soldiers who trained at its Cavalry School served with both the Union and Confederate Armies during the nation's tragic Civil War. When the Confederates invaded the North in 1863, the cavalry forces of Maj. Gen. J. E. B. Stuart occupied

German mercenaries captured at the Battle of Trenton were put to work building the Hessian powder magazine at Carlisle in 1777, which stored gunpowder and munitions for the American troops during the Revolutionary War. Today it serves as a museum of early military history.

the barracks and shelled the town when their demand that the Union defenders surrender was rejected. The Southerners set fire to several buildings at the post. Fortunately for Carlisle, Stuart was immediately ordered to move his cavalry to Gettysburg, where the decisive battle was being fought.

Following the Civil War, the post was rebuilt and became a recruiting depot. In 1871, the army decommissioned Carlisle Barracks and transferred the property to the Department of the Interior for use as the Carlisle Indian Industrial School. During the next thirty-nine years, this innovative vocational school trained 8,000 Indians from 139 tribes and tribal groups in farming, dressmaking, blacksmithing, cooking, metalworking, printing, wagonmaking, and carpentry. Outstanding Indian athletes like Jim Thorpe and Louis Tewanima brought fame to the school in football, baseball, lacrosse, and track.

When World War I began, the army regained possession of the post and used it to rehabilitate wounded soldiers from the front. Later, the Medical Field Service School trained several thousand medical service and noncommissioned officers in battlefield medical care and disease prevention.

During and immediately after World War II, Carlisle Barracks became the home of a number of army schools. In 1951, the Army War

College moved here from Fort Leavenworth, Kansas. Today, the War College prepares selected military, civilian, and international leaders to assume top-level strategic responsibilities. It educates its students on how to deploy U.S. Army units as part of a unified, joint, and multinational force in support of U.S. national military objectives.

WHAT YOU SEE TODAY

Hessian Powder Magazine Museum. This low stone building was constructed in 1777 by Hessian prisoners captured by the Continental Army in the Battle of Trenton. Gunpowder and munitions were stored within its thick limestone walls during the Revolutionary War and the War of 1812. It now houses a museum that depicts the history of Carlisle Barracks. Open daily 10 A.M. to 4 P.M.

Upton Hall. Home of the U.S. Army Military History Institute, which holds some 325,000 books, more than 9,000 bound volumes of periodicals, 1.2 million photographs and more than 7 million unpublished letters, diaries, and memoirs—an outstanding repository of military history from the Colonial era to Operation Desert Storm. These resources are available to historical scholars and family genealogists. The Omar N. Bradley Museum depicts the career of this five-star general who fought in World War II and served as the first chairman of the Joint Chiefs of Staff during the Korean War. The corridors of Upton Hall are decorated with portraits of U.S. Army chiefs of staff and an extensive collection of regimental insignia.

Battle of the Bulge Grove and Monument. See pages 193–94.

Carlisle Indian Industrial School. Several original buildings remain on the grounds from the days of the former Indian school (1879–1918). These buildings are designated as a National Historic Landmark.

When to visit: Monday through Friday, 7:45 A.M. to 4:15 P.M., except federal holidays; Wednesday, 11:30 A.M. to 4:15 P.M.

Admission fees: Free.

Special events: Occasional evening military lectures. Call 717-245-3012 for information.

Tours of the site: A self-guided tour of the post starts at Upton Hall near the front gate. Sign in with the guard and pick up a free booklet with maps and descriptions of the buildings and monuments. To arrange a group tour, call Barracks Public Affairs office, 717-245-4101.

Time needed to visit: Two hours.

Special considerations: Elevator in Upton Hall.

Parking: Free parking nearby on the post.

Gift shop: A bookstore is in nearby Root Hall, which houses the Army War College.

Directions: From the Pennsylvania Turnpike, take the Carlisle interchange to U.S. Route 11 South; from I-81, take the Middlesex exit to U.S. Route 11 South. Go 2 miles to the barracks main gate.

Tourist information

Cumberland Valley Visitor Center, 1255-A Harrisburg Pike, Carlisle, PA 17013, telephone 717-249-4801, website www.parainbow.com.

Other nearby sites

Molly Pitcher Monument and Grave Site. The statue of Mary Ludwig Hays, known as Molly Pitcher, stands in the Old Cemetery near the center of Carlisle. She holds a cannon ramrod in her hands, symbolizing her action on the Revolutionary War battlefield of Monmouth, New Jersey, as she ignored enemy bullets and cannon fire to bring water to American wounded, then took the place of her exhausted and wounded husband as part of the gun crew. She and her husband, William Hays, were natives of Carlisle.

State Museum of Pennsylvania. Within this circular building are four floors of exhibits and displays. Geology, Pennsylvania mammals, natural science and ecology, anthropology, military history, industry and technology, decorative arts, and cultural and educational activities are displayed. The State Archives are open to genealogists and historical scholars. A bookstore offers historical publications on Pennsylvania sites. Located in Harrisburg at Third and North Streets. Admission is free for the museum; a fee is charged for the planetarium. For more information, call 717-787-4978.

USS *Olympia* and USS *Becuna*

Independence Seaport Museum
Penn's Landing
211 South Columbus Boulevard at Walnut Street
Philadelphia, PA 19106-3199.
215-925-5439
fax: 215-925-6713
e-mail: seaport@libertynet.org.
website: www.libertynet.org/~seaport

In the last years of the nineteenth century, Great Britain, France, and Germany were collecting overseas empires in Africa and in Asia. Spain, on the other hand, was desperately trying to hold on to its widespread empire, including Cuba and Puerto Rico, which were both close to the United States.

Americans were becoming increasingly alarmed at the brutal repression being carried out by Spanish authorities as they tried to quell an insurrection against their rule in nearby Cuba. To protect American life and property in Cuba, President William McKinley ordered the battleship *Maine* to Havana Harbor. On February 15, 1898, a huge explosion occurred on the ship, killing 260 of the 350 officers and men on board. The American public, fueled by two partisan newspapers in New York City, was outraged. When an investigative commission reported that the blast could have been caused by a mine in the harbor, many blamed the Spanish. (Many years later, however, it was determined that the explosion was probably caused by the combustion of coal dust in the ship's bunker.) The resulting indignation against Spain swayed public opinion toward those who said that it was the "manifest destiny" of the United States to provide paternalistic leadership for other lands, particularly those that held an economic or military benefit for the United States.

On April 11, 1898, Congress authorized the U.S. armed forces to intervene to install a government of Cubans in place of Spain's colonial rule. On April 21, President McKinley, who had steadfastly tried to avoid war, ordered the U.S. Navy to blockade Havana so supplies could not reach the Spanish. Orders were also sent to the Navy's Asiatic Squadron in Hong Kong to be prepared to attack Spain's Asiatic fleet if war came. On April 25, the House of Representatives voted 310 to 6 to declare war; the Senate concurred, but by a closer vote. On April 26, the United States officially declared war on Spain.

The first action in the newly declared war came not in Cuba, but in the Spanish possession of the Philippines. Comdr. George Dewey lost no time in carrying out his specific orders to "capture or destroy" the Spanish Asiatic fleet. Within five days, his flagship, the protected cruiser *Olympia,* one of America's first steel ships, led a naval attack force of nine ships from the coast of China to Manila Bay, where the Spanish fleet was located.

In order to evade Spanish shore artillery and possible mines, Dewey ordered his ships to steam single file into the harbor under cover of night. In the darkness, the shore batteries fired on the U.S. ships but hit none, and Dewey's squadron succeeded in entering the harbor. Once inside, the American ships steamed slowly across the bay, looking for the Spanish fleet and waiting for dawn to break so crewmen could see

The Spanish-American War comes to Philadelphia with the USS Olympia, *flagship of Comdr. George Dewey, which led the naval attack in Manila Bay. Now berthed at Penn's Landing and open to the visiting public, the restored ship is close to historic sites such as the towering Customs House.*

their targets. Soon they spotted eight Spanish warships lined up at one end of the bay.

Dewey headed directly for the opposing ships, which opened fire on the Americans. When the lead ship, *Olympia,* had closed to 3 miles, Dewey gave the order to the ship's captain, "You may fire when you are ready, Gridley." Then the U.S. warships turned parallel to the line of Spanish ships and opened fire, with telling effect. Five times the U.S. ships moved past the Spanish "sitting ducks," the American shells blasting the opposing ships, causing explosions and starting fires. At one point the Spanish flagship, *Reina Cristina,* got underway to challenge the Americans, but she was hit so hard that she turned and ran herself aground. So one-sided was the Battle of Manila Bay that Dewey ordered the U.S. fleet to take time for breakfast, then went back in action to finish off the Spanish ships and bombard the nearby arsenal.

By noon, not a single Spanish ship remained afloat. The *Olympia* had been hit seven or eight times, but no one on board had been killed. After the battle, the war continued for three more months, as U.S. troops conquered Cuba, Puerto Rico, and the Philippines, with the *Olympia* participating in shelling Manila during the final assault on the capital city.

During the year following the Spanish-American War, the *Olympia* protected American lives and property in Panama, Turkey, and the Dominican Republic. Later she became a training ship for midshipmen of the U.S. Naval Academy.

When World War I broke out, the *Olympia* was designated flagship of the U.S. Patrol Force. She served as an escort for Allied vessels in the North Atlantic and later patrolled for enemy ships off the American coast from New York to Nova Scotia. On June 9, 1918, she landed a peacekeeping force at Murmansk, Russia.

In December 1918, the *Olympia* became flagship of U.S. naval forces in the eastern Mediterranean, where she served as an ambassador of goodwill and a symbol of American strength. One of the cruiser's last assignments came in 1921. On October 3, she was ordered to sail from Plymouth, England, to Le Havre, France. There, with full military honors, she took on board the body of the Unknown Soldier and carried it to its final resting place at Arlington National Cemetery.

Today, the *Olympia* serves as the flagship of Penn's Landing in Philadelphia. As the sole surviving U.S. ship of the Spanish-American War fleet, she is a symbol of the era when the U.S. became a world naval power.

USS Becuna, *a Guppy-type submarine that patrolled the South China Sea and sank two Japanese tankers during World War II, invites visitors to come aboard. She is berthed alongside the USS Olympia at Penn's Landing in Philadelphia.*

The submarine USS *Becuna* (SS-318), named for a pikelike fish found in European waters, was built in 1943. During the final year of World War II in the Pacific, the submersible patrolled the Philippines, South China Sea, and Java Sea looking for Japanese ships. She completed five patrols, sinking two Japanese tankers that totaled 3,888 tons.

In 1949, the *Becuna* went through the Panama Canal to join the Atlantic Fleet as a unit of Submarine Squadron 8, conducting refresher training exercises and training student officers and enlisted men at New London, Connecticut. In 1950, she was converted to a streamlined fast underwater submarine, known as a Guppy 1A type. The addition of a German-type snorkel air system allowed her to increase her diesel engines' underwater speed. Other additions included the installation of a large electric battery for longer underwater endurance, sophisticated radar, fire control, and torpedo equipment, including nuclear warheads.

She then rejoined the Atlantic Fleet, twice taking part in patrols and exercises with the U.S. Sixth Fleet in the Mediterranean Sea. She ended her career as a training submarine at New London and was decommissioned in 1969.

WHAT YOU SEE TODAY

The USS *Olympia*, still painted in the traditional buff and white of her era, is berthed at Penn's Landing alongside the USS *Becuna*. Both ships are maintained by the Independence Seaport Museum, which interprets maritime history with a variety of permanent and interactive exhibits and a workshop in which small boats are built.

Visitors may go aboard both the cruiser and the submarine. On board the *Olympia*, visitors may walk from the bridge to the engine room, inspect the fashionable wooden paneling in the wardroom, watch crewmen fire one of her smaller cannons, and learn from volunteer guides how the ship was sailed. Life-size figures in some compartments set the scene and add to the realism. Display cases hold Spanish-American War memorabilia. Two footprints at one side of the bridge show where Capt. Charles V. Gridley stood when Commodore Dewey gave him the order to fire at the Spanish ships in Manila Bay.

On board the *Becuna* a guide takes small groups below decks into the 312-foot submarine to describe the daily life of its eighty-man crew. They see where the crew members ate and slept and how they spent their time during long patrols at sea. Visitors learn how a submarine dives, how it produces electricity and fresh water, how it operates its radar and sonar equipment, and how it fires its torpedoes.

When to visit: Daily, 10 A.M. to 5 P.M.

Admission fees: Adults $7.50, seniors $6, children $3.50; includes USS *Becuna*, USS *Olympia*, and the museum.

Special events: On occasion, uniformed reenactors man the ship and give guided tours and flag and gunnery demonstrations. From time to time, band concerts are held aboard.

Tours of the site: The tour of the cruiser is self-guided; guided tours are given of the submarine.

Time needed to visit: Four hours for all three sites.

Special considerations: Full mobility required to negotiate steep stairs and cramped quarters on both the submarine and the cruiser.

Parking: At Penn's Landing for a fee.

Gift shop: Books, periodicals, nautical gift items, and memorabilia.

Directions: From I-95 North or South, take exit 16. Turn left on Columbus Boulevard, then turn right under the Walnut Street pedestrian bridge into the Penn's Landing parking lot.

Other nearby sites

See Independence National Historical Park (pages 53–56).

Pennsylvania Military Museum

U.S. Business Route 322
P.O. Box 148
Boalsburg, PA 16827
814-466-6263
fax: 814-466-6616
e-mail: wleech@phmc.state.pa.us
website: www.psu.edu/dept/aerospace/museum/

The Pennsylvania Military Museum is located at the site where officers of the 28th Infantry Division returned after World War I to hold their division reunions and to place memorials to their fallen comrades. Earlier, the site had been a training ground for Col. Theodore Boal's mounted machine gun troop. Boal was a diplomat and an early advocate of preparedness for the United States.

The 28th Division, one of the components of the Pennsylvania National Guard, was federalized in 1917 and sent to fight with the Allied forces in Europe. Colonel Boal's privately raised machine gun troop became Company A of the 107th Machine Gun Battalion of the 28th Division. When the division returned after the war, it resumed its previous status as part of the state's National Guard, which it remains to this day.

The museum is part of a 66-acre park built on land previously owned by the Boal family, early landowners in the area. Nearby is the 28th Division Shrine, which contains monuments and memorials that commemorate the sacrifice of generations of Pennsylvania servicemen and pays honor to other Pennsylvania military units, dating back to Benjamin Franklin's first volunteer unit in the Revolutionary War, the Associators.

Exhibits in the museum building trace the evolution of Pennsylvania's citizen-soldiers from the early years and describe the formation of the National Guard in 1870–71. A weapons gallery traces the development of automatic weapons, from the Gatling gun to the .50-caliber Colt machine gun.

The centerpiece of the museum is a full-scale replica of a World War I trench system, with life-size figures of uniformed soldiers shown at battle positions. The sounds of battle and flashes simulating gunfire add realism to the scene for the visitor. Nearby is a grim reminder of the cost of battle—a forward first aid post and a field ambulance.

The Pennsylvania Military Museum at Boalsburg gives visitors a firsthand look at Pennsylvania's military heritage from Colonial days to Operation Desert Storm. Alongside the museum is the shrine to Pennsylvania's 28th Infantry Division. The nation's first Memorial Day was celebrated in Boalsburg in 1864.

Another gallery, devoted to the experience of Pennsylvania soldiers, sailors, airmen, and marines in World War II, the Korean War, and the Vietnam War, includes clothing and equipment, as well as narratives of individuals of all ranks and services who played roles in combat and command.

WHAT YOU SEE TODAY
The museum is administered by the Pennsylvania Historical and Museum Commission. War weapons, including artillery pieces, caissons, and a World War II Sherman tank, are displayed on the grounds outside the museum building.

28th Division Shrine. Pathways lead past monuments and memorials in a park that commemorates the service of the 28th Division in World War II.

When to visit: April to October, Tuesday through Saturday, 9 A.M. to 5 P.M.; Sunday, 12 noon to 5 P.M. November through March, reduced hours—call for appointment. Open Memorial Day, July 4, and Labor Day.

Admission fees: Adults $3.50, seniors $3.00, children $1.50.

Special events: Third weekend in May: Armed Forces Weekend, a celebration service honoring all Pennsylvania veterans, including a concert, helicopter and vehicle displays, and notable speakers; Memorial Day weekend: encampment of World War II reenactment troops and demonstrations; July: People's Choice Festival of Pennsylvania Arts.

Tours of the site: Self-guided.

Time needed to visit: Two hours.

Special considerations: Museum building and shrine are handicapped-accessible.

Parking: Free.

Gift shop: Books, military artwork, souvenirs, and memorabilia.

Directions: Three miles east of State College on U.S. Business Route 322 in Boalsburg.

Tourist information

Centre County Convention and Visitor Bureau—Penn State Country, 1402 South Atherton Street, State College, PA 16801, telephone 814-231-1400 or 800-358-5466, website www.visitpennstate.org.

Other nearby sites

Columbus Chapel and Boal Mansion Museum. The strongest connection to Christopher Columbus in the United States. The Columbus Chapel was brought to the Boal Estate from Spain in 1909. Columbus family heirlooms and archives date back to the 1400s, including his admiral's desk. The Boal Mansion displays decorative arts and furnishings of nine generations of this family's international ancestry. Located on Business Route 322, the museum is open for tours May through October. For more information, call 814-466-6210.

Soldiers and Sailors
Memorial Hall

4141 Fifth Avenue (at Bigelow Boulevard)
Oakland
Pittsburgh, PA 15213
412-621-4253
fax: 412-683-9339
e-mail: curator_ssmh@yahoo.com
website: www.soldiersandsailorshall.org

This monumental structure near the University of Pittsburgh was built in 1910 by the Grand Army of the Republic, an organization of veterans of the Civil War, to recognize the service of men from Allegheny County to their country. Its purpose later expanded, and today it honors Pennsylvania soldiers, sailors, airmen, and marines, from the Civil War to the Persian Gulf War.

The edifice is styled after the ancient mausoleum of Halicarnassus, one of the Seven Wonders of the Ancient World. It is listed on the National Register of Historic Places. The original building in Greece is the tomb of the Persian governor Mausolus, who died in the fifth century B.C.

The museum occupies a 4-acre site within walking distance of several other Pittsburgh landmarks: the University of Pittsburgh's Cathedral of Learning, Heinz Chapel, Carnegie Library and Museum, Carnegie Mellon University, Hillman Library, and the University of Pittsburgh Medical Center.

WHAT YOU SEE TODAY

Exhibits are displayed on two floors, in cases placed in the wide corridors that encircle the central 2,500-seat auditorium on the first floor and a banquet hall on the second floor. Bronze plaques on the walls list the names of 25,920 Pennsylvania soldiers who fought in the Civil War.

A Hall of Valor honors Allegheny County veterans who earned America's highest awards for valor in combat, from the Silver Star to the Medal of Honor. Exhibits include a collection of rifles and pistols from the 1840s to the 1960s. One pistol in the collection has an unusual history. It was an American-made pistol that was captured from a U.S.

186

officer by a German soldier during World War I. Years later, in 1943, when the 78th Division fought in the Battle of the Bulge, its soldiers captured a German officer, who surrendered his pistol. This turned out to be the same World War I American-made pistol.

Other exhibits show captured war trophies from Germany, Japan, and Iraq; Civil War displays that include rifles, swords, uniforms, and memorabilia; a World War I display of helmets, gas masks, carved shell casings, and rare uniforms; a Korean War exhibit that includes a 60mm mortar; and weapons used in Vietnam by the Viet Cong forces.

Visitors also view a 16-foot-long model of the USS *Pittsburgh* (CA 72), a World War II U.S. Navy heavy cruiser, and a submarine torpedo. Another exhibit describes the roles servicewomen played during World War I and World War II.

Genealogical or historical researchers may use the museum's 3,000-volume research library. Archival collections include a wide range of papers and photographs. The library also holds numerous Civil War records and diaries.

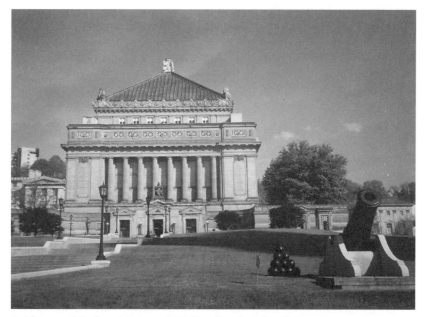

Soldiers and Sailors Memorial Hall in Pittsburgh exhibits weapons, war trophies, uniforms, and memorabilia from U.S. wars, from the Civil War to the Persian Gulf War.

When to visit: Monday through Friday, 9 A.M. to 4 P.M.; Saturday and Sunday, 1 P.M. to 4 P.M.

Admission fees: Free; donations accepted.

Special events: October: Dedication Day, when Civil War reenactors stage an encampment on the museum's broad front lawn, demonstrating their weapons and equipment. Costumed guides, band music, history talks, and entertainment add to the event. Museum staff members also visit local schools with military equipment and uniform items.

Tours of the site: Self-guided. Guided tours: adults $3, children $1.

Time needed to visit: One hour.

Special considerations: Accessible by elevator.

Parking: In an underground garage beneath the museum for a fee.

Gift shop: Books, memorabilia, and souvenirs for sale.

Directions: From the Pennsylvania Turnpike (I-76), take I-376 West to the Oakland exit. Continue in right lane up hill to second traffic light, turn left, then turn right at next traffic light onto Forbes Avenue. Turn left on Bigelow Boulevard to museum.

Other nearby sites

See Fort Pitt Museum (pages 16–17).

Camp Colt

Gettysburg National Military Park
97 Taneytown Road
Gettysburg, PA 17325
717-334-1124
website: www.nps.gov.gett/

It had been almost a year since the United States had entered World War I, and the U.S. Army needed camps to train the many new enlistees who rushed to the colors. Capt. Dwight Eisenhower, just three years out of West Point, had organized a tank battalion in Texas. Now, in March 1918, he was ordered to establish a training camp for future tank corps soldiers at the site of an abandoned National Guard camp at Gettysburg. Oddly enough, the location of the camp was to be right in the middle of what is now preserved as hallowed ground by Gettysburg National Military Park—the site of the tragic Pickett's Charge by Confederate forces during the Battle of Gettysburg on July 3, 1863 (see pages 160–66).

It was the young captain's first command, although his real desire was to go overseas where the war was being fought. "My personal orders were specific," Eisenhower later wrote. "I was required to take in volunteers, equip, organize and instruct them and have them ready for overseas shipment when called upon."

The new camp was named for Samuel Colt, the inventor of the Colt revolver. Tents were set up in the spring of 1918, covering acres of land in the midst of the Gettysburg battlefield. Photographs show a mass of tents, as well as several wooden barracks.

To keep the men busy, Eisenhower had them drill on the parade ground. He also introduced physical conditioning and had them learn Morse code and telegraphy. The men of Camp Colt viewed Eisenhower as a strict disciplinarian who demanded that they work hard toward perfection. He chided the troops for "showing a lack of the snap and precision which must characterize close order drill." Despite his strong emphasis on discipline, he was careful to look out for his men's well-being.

With limited supplies and equipment, Eisenhower found other ways to train and care for his men. Motor schools were established to train them in engine repair. Machine guns were mounted on trucks and flatbeds so that the men could practice firing from moving vehicles and at moving targets. By midsummer, the camp had grown to nearly 10,000 men and 600 officers.

Eisenhower obtained a few small-caliber cannons, similar to the ones used on tanks, and drilled with these. Finally, the camp received three French tanks, and the would-be tank soldiers got a chance to see the armament they would one day be called upon to operate. According to the local newspaper, the men "were as happy as a playground full of children with a new toy."

After dispatching several groups of trained soldiers to Europe, Camp Colt was closed and its trainees transferred to North Carolina when the onset of winter made living in tents at Gettysburg impractical. Eisenhower finally received the orders he had been asking for—to command a group of soldiers who would be sent to the European front lines. But

NATIONAL PARK SERVICE

Capt. Dwight Eisenhower (left) as the commandant, introduces three visiting officers to Camp Colt in 1918. The basic mission of the camp was to prepare World War I recruits for combat duty with the Army Tank Corps in Europe.

NATIONAL PARK SERVICE

Camp Colt in 1918 sprawled across terrain once covered by Pickett's Charge during the Battle of Gettysburg. (Note the dome of the Pennsylvania State Memorial on the horizon.) The scene has since been restored to its appearance at the time of the battle, and nothing remains of the World War I camp but a historical marker.

before his reassignment could go through, the war ended, with Germany signing the armistice on November 11, 1918.

More than twenty years later, during World War II, a section of the Pickett's Charge area was temporarily used once more—this time to hold captured German prisoners of war who were assigned to Gettysburg. The prisoners were soon moved to a former Civilian Conservation Corps camp nearby and sent to help local farmers harvest their crops.

WHAT YOU SEE TODAY

Historical Marker. The only evidence remaining of Camp Colt today is a marker indicating its location near the Codori Farm on Emmitsburg Road. Earlier, the Codori Farm had been a landmark during the third day of the Battle of Gettysburg. The location is marked by a sign and a tree planted in soil from each of the forty-eight states. The sign was erected in 1954 by the World Wars Tank Corps Association to honor the inauguration of Dwight D. Eisenhower as 34th President of the United States.

Tours of the site: Self-guided.

Time needed to visit: Quarter hour.

Special events: Memorial Day weekend: Camp Colt Weekend, with encampment of reenactment troops in World War I–style tents at the nearby Eisenhower National Historic Site. Reenactors portray doughboys in training, as well as members of the Red Cross, YMCA, and Salvation Army, who accompanied the troops. An exhibit portrays the early history of the U.S. Army Tank Corps.

Parking: Roadside parking for the historic marker.

Directions: Gettysburg is located at the junction of U.S. Route 30 and U.S. Route 15. From exit 17 of the Pennsylvania Turnpike, travel south 30 miles on U.S. Route 15 to exit for Steinwehr Avenue. Follow signs to the park. Camp Colt historic marker is .5 miles south of park entrance on Steinwehr Avenue (Emmitsburg Road).

Other nearby sites

See Gettysburg National Military Park (page 154).

Battle of the Bulge Monuments

Public Affairs Office
Military History Institute
U.S. Army War College
122 Forbes Avenue
Carlisle Barracks, PA 17013-5234
717-245-3971
fax: 717-245-3711
e-mail: awcc-dmh@awc.carlisle.mil
website: carlisle-www.army.mil

Pennsylvania Department of Military and Veterans Affairs
Fort Indiantown Gap
Annville, PA 17003-5002
717-861-8829
fax: 717-861-8211

Valley Forge Military Academy and College
1001 Eagle Road
Wayne, PA 19087
610-989-1200
fax: 610-989-1487
website: www.VFMAC.edu

Three monuments in Pennsylvania commemorate the World War II Allied victory in the Battle of the Bulge, fought from December 1944 to January 1945. More than 600,000 U.S. soldiers took part in what was the largest land battle ever fought by the U.S. Army.

The monuments recall the German Army's largest offensive against the Western allies, which took place near the border between Belgium and Luxembourg in the Ardennes region. The battle got its name from the huge bulge the Germans made in the American lines before they were pushed back in six weeks of desperate combat in the midst of a brutal winter. For the first three days, six U.S. divisions defended their ground against thirty German divisions, until powerful U.S. reinforcements arrived.

The Americans suffered 81,000 casualties, including 19,000 killed; the British had 1,400 casualties, with 200 killed; and the Germans sustained 100,000 casualties. "This is undoubtedly the greatest Ameri-

193

can battle of the war," said wartime British prime minister Winston Churchill, "and will, I believe, be regarded as an ever famous American victory."

WHAT YOU SEE TODAY

Battle of the Bulge Grove and Monument. A monument on the campus of the U.S. Army War College, in Carlisle, honors the soldiers who lost their lives in this last major battle in the Western European theater of World War II. The monument is located in a large park and is surrounded by a grove of fir trees, which are common in the Ardennes forest (see pages 173–77).

Battle of the Bulge Monument. A black-and-white marble monument commemorating the battle stands at a major road junction within the National Guard base at Fort Indiantown Gap in Annville. Presented by the World War II Historical Preservation Federation, the monument is dedicated to "the six hundred thousand American men and women, who in World War II fought three German armies in the Ardennes Forest of Belgium and Luxembourg and won the largest land battle ever fought by the U.S. Army" (see pages 197–200).

In 1999 M.Sgt. Jules Desgain, who fought with the 28th Infantry Division in the Battle of the Bulge in 1944, was selected to unveil the battle's newest memorial at Fort Indiantown Gap. Desgain not only is a veteran of the actual battle, but also takes part in World War II battle reenactments.

VALLEY FORGE MILITARY ACADEMY, DAVID JACKSON

Cadet Capt. David Esquela of Valley Forge Military Academy and Junior College pays homage to the Battle of the Bulge Monument located on the academy grounds in Wayne.

World War II Battle of the Bulge International Monument. This monument, titled *A Triumph of Courage*, at Valley Forge Military Academy and College, in Wayne, is the only memorial in the country that flies the flags of the United States, Belgium, and Luxembourg twenty-four hours a day. The flags, illuminated at night, recall the sacrifices of the heroic people of Belgium and Luxembourg, who had their freedom restored by the Allied victory after four years of German occupation. The monument was erected with funds contributed by veterans and their families and friends, with significant donations from the governments and people of Belgium and Luxembourg.

When to visit: Tourists may visit Valley Forge Military Academy and College weekdays, Saturday, and Sunday, 9 A.M. to 5 P.M.
Admission fees: Free.
Special events: Memorial Day, Veterans Day, and December 16 (the day the battle started): veterans of the Battle of the Bulge services at 11 A.M.

Tours of the site: Self-guided.

Time needed to visit: Half hour.

Special considerations: Site is handicapped accessible.

Parking: Free.

Directions: Take exit 24 off the Pennsylvania Turnpike. After the toll-booth, take second exit, Route 202 South. Follow sign for Warner Road to first traffic light. Turn left onto Warner Road, and proceed 1 mile to stop sign. Turn right onto Croton Road, and follow it approximately .25 mile to first left, Radnor Road. Follow Radnor Road across one intersection to Valley Forge Military Academy and College and its parade ground.

Other nearby sites

See Valley Forge National Historical Park (pages 98–99).

Fort Indiantown Gap

Pennsylvania Department of Military and Veterans Affairs
Fort Indiantown Gap
Annville, PA 17003-5002
717-861-8468
fax: 717-861-8211

Fort Indiantown Gap, an expansive military post located 20 miles northeast of Harrisburg, serves as the headquarters of the Pennsylvania Army and the Air National Guard. The National Guard forces share a dual federal-state responsibility. Members are trained and equipped to join the active military forces in time of war or national emergency. And the National Guard takes orders from the governor if required to protect lives and property during disasters, civil disturbances, or threats to the public health.

The base, originally named Indiantown Gap Military Reservation, was officially designated in 1975 as Fort Indiantown Gap. Land was first purchased for the base in 1931, when the Pennsylvania National Guard needed a larger area for training maneuvers and firing and bombing ranges than the military reservation it was then using at Mount Gretna. Additional land was purchased, bringing the total to more than 18,000 acres. The National Guard first held training maneuvers at the base in 1933.

With Europe engaged in World War II and the United States preparing for the possibility of entering the conflict, Pennsylvania agreed in September 1940 to lease its National Guard post to the U.S. Army for a training base. A massive construction program rapidly converted the post into an extensive military base. Over the next year, more than 13,000 workmen constructed more than 1,400 buildings, including hundreds of barracks, many small-arms ranges, a field artillery range 7.5 miles long, an airfield and hangars, several lakes used by the troops to practice amphibious landings, numerous dining halls, nine chapels, and a 400-bed hospital. Seven U.S. Army divisions received their preparation here to be shipped to Europe and the Southwest Pacific to fight with the Allied forces.

After the victory in Europe, the base became a separation center to demobilize the servicemen as they returned home. By mid-September 1945, the discharge rate reached 1,000 soldiers a day. The next month, the center was processing 3,000 or more soldiers each day. One army

Four U.S. "infantrymen" dismount from their jeep to search for "German" positions during a World War II reenactment of the Battle of the Bulge at Fort Indiantown Gap.

authority estimates that 250,000 soldiers passed through the base on their way to battle Nazi Germany and Japan; some 450,000 were processed through the camp on their way home after the war.

After its use as a separation center, the post once again reverted to the Pennsylvania National Guard and Air National Guard. In 1951, the federal government again assumed control, using the post as an active U.S. Army base during the Korean War. Here the army trained 32,000 men of the 5th Infantry Division as replacements for other army divisions fighting in Korea.

Following the Korean War, the post once more became the headquarters and training area for the Pennsylvania National Guard. Today, the military post comprises 19,200 acres, or about 30 square miles. Its buildings include numerous barracks to house troops, permanent headquarters buildings, maintenance shops, supply warehouses, an Army Reserve Training Center, a large sports complex, and a large training complex with an educational building, dormitories, and a dining hall. The post also has an artillery range, a tank firing range, a large ammunition storage area, an armory, and a helicopter training facility. Pilots practice bombing and rocketry at an air-to-ground bombing range.

On two other occasions, Fort Indiantown Gap was pressed into service for humanitarian instead of military purposes. In 1975, the post was used to temporarily house 32,000 Vietnamese and Cambodian refugees evacuated from the Far East until they could be sponsored and resettled elsewhere in the United States. In 1980, it became a refugee camp again when 19,000 Cuban aliens were brought here for processing and resettlement.

Each January, Fort Indiantown Gap holds an elaborate reenactment of the Battle of the Bulge of World War II. Under the leadership of the World War II Historical Preservation Federation, more than 1,000 reenactors maneuver over the post's terrain using privately owned tanks, jeeps, trucks—even German motorcycle sidecars—as they reenact a mock Battle of the Bulge using blank bullets and shells. Reenactors play both American and German soldiers in these realistic exercises.

WHAT YOU SEE TODAY

Pennsylvania National Guard Military Museum. The museum is housed in a barracks typical of those used by troops awaiting embarkation to Europe during World War II. At one end of the museum is a scene depicting how soldiers lived in the barracks. Other exhibits display photographs, uniforms, and equipment used by soldiers in conflicts from the Civil War to Desert Storm. Two World War I German machine guns and a Gatling gun are on exhibit, as is a model of a U.S. Sherman tank made by a German prisoner who was interned at Indiantown Gap during World War II. Outside is a U.S. tank once used in battle.

Post Airfield. This is the largest Reserve Component helicopter training facility in the United States, and includes four state-of-the-art simulators. Observers may watch as National Guard pilots practice helicopter takeoffs and landings at Muir Army Field. About seventy-five helicopters are based at the field.

Friendship Train Monument. In the center of the post is a French railway boxcar, a gift from France to the people of Pennsylvania. This "Boxcar Memorial" is part of France's response to a "Friendship Train" of food, clothing, and medical supplies donated by the American people to France and Italy in the aftermath of World War II. In 1949, the French responded with a "Gratitude Train" to the United States, which included a boxcar for each state loaded with products of France. The boxcar is one of the stubby "40 and 8" (forty men or eight horses) French boxcars that became familiar to U.S. soldiers in France during

World War I. On its sides are painted the coats of arms of the forty French provinces.

Battle of the Bulge Monument. See page 194. Nearby stand monuments to the 95th Infantry Division, the 28th Infantry Division, and the 3rd Armored Division. An F-102 Delta Dagger, an all-weather fighter-interceptor aircraft, is also displayed.

Lieutenant Governor's residence. A fieldstone home near the main entrance to the post, the mansion was built in 1947 as the home of the governor. In 1972, a new governor's mansion was built in Harrisburg, and today the lieutenant governor of the state resides here with his family. It is not open to the public.

Indiantown Gap National Cemetery. Located adjacent to Fort Indiantown Gap, on Fort Indiantown Gap Road near exit 29 from I-81, the national cemetery holds the remains of 15,000 U.S. veterans and their dependents. The cemetery, one of 115 national cemeteries in the nation, covers 677 acres of rolling countryside and has headstones flush with the ground. Its administration building resembles a Pennsylvania Dutch–style barn and has an observation area and a carillon. Flags line the entrance road from Memorial Day to July 4 each year as well as on Veterans Day.

When to visit: Daily, 9 A.M. to 5 P.M.
Admission fees: Free.
Special events: January: World War II Battle of the Bulge reenactment.
Tours of the site: Self-guided.
Time needed to visit: Three hours.
Special considerations: Handicapped accessible.
Parking: Free.
Directions: Take exit 29 off I-81. Follow PA Route 934 North a short distance to the base entrance.

Tourist information
 PA Rainbow Region Vacation Bureau, 625 Quentin Road, Lebanon, PA 17402, telephone 717-261-1200, website www.parainbow.com.

USS *Requin*

Riverside at the Carnegie Science Center
1 Allegheny Avenue
Pittsburgh, PA 15212-5850
412-237-3400 or 412-237-1550
website: www.csc.clpgh.org

This World War II U.S. Navy submarine, named for a sand shark species, was built in 1945. After its shakedown off the New England coast, the submarine went through the Panama Canal to the Pacific. Since it reached Pearl Harbor two weeks before the war in the Pacific ended, the USS *Requin* saw no battle action.

In 1946, the Navy converted the submarine into its first radar picket ship, removing its rear torpedo tubes and replacing them with radar-detection equipment designed to detect and track long-range missiles. A snorkel system was installed that allowed the submarine to run on diesel power while submerged to a depth of 52 feet. *Requin* was then reclassified as SSR-481.

In 1949, she operated in the western Atlantic Ocean, ranging from Nova Scotia to the West Indies. From 1950 to 1957, she rotated duty stations between the Mediterranean Sea, where she operated with the U.S. Sixth Fleet, and the U.S. east coast, where she operated with the Second Fleet.

In 1958, the USS *Requin* was reclassified as SS-481 when she was fitted with a high fiberglass sail to improve her surface visibility. The ship conducted local operations from the naval base at Norfolk, Virginia, cruising in the western Atlantic and Caribbean Sea. In 1966, the submarine sailed to South America for exercises with various South American navies and was deployed for the last time with the Sixth Fleet in the Mediterranean.

Decommissioned in 1968, the USS *Requin* became a Naval Reserve training ship in St. Petersburg, Florida, until 1971, when the Navy transferred the ship to the city of Tampa. The Carnegie Science Center acquired the submarine in 1990, towing it up the Mississippi River and berthing it in the Ohio River at the museum.

WHAT YOU SEE TODAY

A guide, usually a U.S. Navy veteran, takes visitors belowdecks to see how a World War II submarine operated, where they learn about the

USS Requin, *a radar picket submarine during World War II and the Cold War, is moored in the Ohio River as part of the Carnegie Science Center in Pittsburgh.*

daily life of the eighty-one-man crew—where they ate and slept and how they passed the time during long patrols at sea—as well as how a submarine dives, produces electricity and fresh water, operates its radar equipment, fires its torpedoes, tracks enemy vessels, and secretly prowls the ocean depths, eluding detection by the enemy. They learn how radar devices see through fog and rain, listen to sonar signals pinpointing objects miles away, and find out how sonar specialists distinguish between enemy vessels and whales and other underwater objects.

When to visit: Spring and fall, Monday through Saturday, 9 A.M. to 4:30 P.M.; Sunday, 10 A.M. to 5:30 P.M. Summer, daily, 10 A.M. to 5:30 P.M. Winter, Saturday and Sunday, 10 A.M. to 4:30 P.M.

Admission fees: Adults $4, seniors and children $2.

Tours of the site: Guided tours by former Navy sailors.

Time needed to visit: One hour.

Special considerations: Full mobility required to negotiate steep stairways and cramped quarters.

Parking: At the Carnegie Science Center for a fee.

Gift shop: Books, periodicals, nautical gift items, and memorabilia.

Directions: From downtown Pittsburgh, take the Fort Duquesne Bridge toward Three Rivers Stadium. Drive West on U.S. Route 65, and follow signs to Carnegie Science Center.

Mid-Atlantic Air Museum

Reading Regional Airport
11 Museum Drive
Reading, PA 19605
610-372-7333
fax: 610-372-1702
e-mail: russ@maam.org
website: www.maam.org

Visitors to the Mid-Atlantic Air Museum on the first weekend in June will find themselves immersed in the 1939–45 era. This is the World War II Weekend, the museum's big event of the year, a history lesson on which it devotes much of its efforts throughout the year. Here visitors can experience the war years as they view realistic living-history reenactments of land warfare; wander through an extensive tent city where U.S., Canadian, British, Irish, and German troops encamp for the weekend, displaying and demonstrating their equipment and vehicles; and watch vintage World War II fighter planes, bombers, transport planes, and trainers fly by. The rest of the time, these planes are parked on the apron, where visitors can take a close-up look.

In reenactments, a forward field surgical unit in a large tent operates on several wounded casualties that have been brought in on stretchers from the battle area; a U.S. rifle platoon supported by armored vehicles moves to drive German infantrymen from an airfield and thus secure it for the Allied forces; and German soldiers in a French village capture a U.S. flier who has been forced to parachute from his damaged aircraft; soldiers of the 1st Infantry Division repair small arms, clean rifles and machine guns, and tune up army motorcycles, while a Women's Army Corps (WAC) detachment stocks spare parts and keeps them moving to the men of the repair division.

Jeeps, armored vehicles, motorcycles, and civilian antique cars thread their way through the crowds that throng the apron of the Mid-Atlantic Air Museum at the Carl A. Spaatz Field, a portion of the Reading Regional Airport. Visitors see officers and soldiers in World War II uniforms; women in the uniforms of the WAC, WAVES, WAF, and Women Marines; and men and women dressed in civilian fashions of the 1940s. Impersonators of President Franklin D. Roosevelt, his wife, Eleanor, and Lt. Gen. George Patton play their historic roles.

Fearless visitors to the Mid-Atlantic Air Museum in Reading may go aloft in this venerable N3N-3 open-cockpit biplane. Designed in 1934, the Yellow Peril was once used to train U.S. Navy fliers.

At one recent World War II Weekend, Bob Morgan and Jim Verinis, pilot and copilot of the B-17 bomber *Memphis Belle*, the first B-17 to complete twenty-five bombing missions over France, Belgium, and Germany, met the public. So did Fred Olivi, who was the copilot of the B-29 bomber *Enola Gay*, which dropped the atomic bomb on Nagasaki, Japan, in the closing days of the war. On hand as well were five members of the Flying Tigers, a group of volunteer airmen who flew supplies over the Himalaya Mountains to the forces of the Chinese Nationalists.

The Air Museum is open the rest of the year as well, housed in a former hangar of the Reading Airport. More than twenty-one aircraft are on display, either in the hangar or outside on the airstrip. Others are in storage, ready for future restoration. Air Museum planes appear at some thirty air shows each year, and the crewmen often give tours to air-show visitors. Visitors may take a flight in either an AT6/SNJ Texan trainer or an open-cockpit N3N Yellow Peril biplane for a fee.

An ongoing project is the reconstruction of a P-61 Black Widow night fighter plane that the museum retrieved from a crash site in New Guinea in 1961. The P-61 has a powerful radar system in its nose, plus a unique, twin-fuselage design and slotted flaps and ailerons that enabled it to operate from a short airstrip. The museum expects the plane to once again be flown; if it is, it will be the only P-61 in the world in operating condition.

WHAT YOU SEE TODAY

The Air Museum is in a hangar at one side of the Reading Regional Airport. During World War II, the hangar housed B-24 Liberator bombers that were being prepared to be ferried to England. Later, it became the headquarters of the first Pennsylvania Air National Guard unit.

Besides the restored aircraft, the museum also houses a number of exhibits on aviation history.

When to visit: Open daily, 9:30 A.M. to 4 P.M.
Admission fees: Adults $5, children $2.
Special events: First weekend in June: World War II Weekend.
Tours of the site: Self-guided; volunteer guides sometimes available.
Time needed to visit: One hour.
Special considerations: Handicapped accessible.
Parking: Free.
Gift shop: Aircraft memorabilia.
Directions: Take exit 21 off the Pennsylvania Turnpike (I-76), and get on U.S. Route 222 North. Take PA Route 183 West, toward the Reading Regional Airport. Turn right on Van Reed Road (SR 3055), and follow blue-and-white museum signs to the museum.

Tourist information
Reading and Berks County Visitor Bureau, 352 Penn Street, Reading, PA 19610, telephone 610-375-4085 or 800-443-6610, website www.readingberkspa.com.

Other nearby sites
Schuylkill River Heritage Corridor. One of nine state heritage regions. Follows the 128 meandering miles of the Schuylkill River through five counties, encompassing sites that tell the story of anthracite coal shipped via river barges, fertile agriculture, and the charcoal-fired industries that brought wealth to Philadelphia. Historic homes, museums, and landmarks help tell the story. For more information, call 610-372-3916.

Berks County Heritage Center. Includes the restored nineteenth-century Gruber Wagon Works, where original tools and equipment are displayed. The center also traces the history of transportation on the Union and Schuylkill Canals through exhibits at the Howard Heister Canal Center. Visitors may hike the 5-mile-long Union Canal Trail on the grounds. The center is located 5 miles northwest of Reading via Route 183 and Red Bridge Road. Open from May 1 through October, Tuesday through Saturday. Admission fee. For more information, call 610-374-8839.

INDEX